U.S. Government and Presidents

Grades 3-5

by Amy Gamble

Carson-Dellosa Publishing Company, Inc.
Greensboro, North Carolina

Credits

Project Director: Jennifer Weaver-Spencer

Editor: Carrie Fox

Layout Design: Tiara Reynolds

Inside Illustrations: Jenny Campbell

Cover Design: Peggy Jackson

Cover Art: Tara Tavonatti

This book has been correlated to state, national, and Canadian provincial standards. Visit *www.carsondellosa.com* to search for and view its correlations to your standards.

ISBN 978-1-60418-602-4
05-214161151

Table of Contents

Introduction

U.S. Government and Presidents is organized into 13 sections of related topics. The first section of worksheets introduces students to the idea of government, including the different types of government and the purposes government serves. The next sections cover the ideals, symbols, and history of the U.S. government. Next are sections about the Constitution and the three branches of government. After students become familiar with the federal government, they will learn about the aspects of government that most citizens are familiar with—state and local government, paying taxes, voting, and citizenship. The final section includes information and activities about each U.S. president.

The activities in the book are designed to be fun and informative, and do not have to be completed in any particular order. If desired, students can use the Internet or other resources to research certain topics in more detail. Students may work on the activities as a class or in small groups to stimulate discussions or debates. You may even wish to place several pages at a center each week, along with reference materials for students to complete independently.

As you present the activities in this book, help students understand that acquiring knowledge about history and government is an important part of being a good citizen.

Government in Your Life

Every day you see government at work. No, you're not on Capitol Hill watching laws being made, but as you walk or drive around your city or town, you can see the effects of laws, regulations, and services that the government provides.

Look at the scene below. Circle each area in the picture where you see the effects of government. Then, choose one area you circled and explain what effect government has in that area.

_____

_____

_____

_____

_____

_____

What Is Government?

Government is all of the agencies, departments, organizations, groups, and individuals in a nation who make, carry out, enforce, and manage conflicts about rules and laws. Government is like a nation's family. Families take care of children and make sure they are safe, healthy, educated, and free to enjoy life. Families encourage children to be independent, hardworking, and responsible. Families make and enforce rules and give appropriate punishments when rules are broken. Government does these things for its citizens, too.

Answer the questions below to show how government is like a family. Use a separate sheet of paper if necessary.

1. How does your family keep you safe? _____

_____

2. How does the government keep its citizens safe? _____

_____

3. How does your family keep you healthy? _____

_____

4. How does the government keep its citizens healthy? _____

_____

5. How does your family help you learn and become educated?

_____

6. How does the government help its citizens learn and become educated?

_____

7. What kinds of rules does your family have for you? _____

_____

8. What kinds of rules does the government have for its citizens?

_____

9. How does your family punish you if you break the rules? _____

_____

10. How does the government punish its citizens who break the law? _____

_____

Authority vs. Power

If someone has power, he or she can direct or control a person or thing. If someone has authority, he or she has been given the right to have and use power. Authority is given to someone through customs, laws, or consent. Laws (the Constitution) and the consent (elections) of the American people give the United States government the authority to make and enforce laws.

For each situation below, explain whether the person in power has authority.

1. Your family takes away your video games until your grades improve.

_____

2. A crossing guard stops traffic so that children can walk across the street.

_____

3. A masked robber holds up a bank and steals money.

_____

4. A bully takes lunch money from other children on her bus.

_____

5. Your friend takes your pencil after you tell him that he can borrow it.

_____

6. A teacher tells his students to work quietly.

_____

7. A boy hits another boy on the playground.

_____

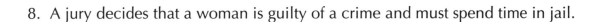

8. A jury decides that a woman is guilty of a crime and must spend time in jail.

_____

9. A woman puts up a stop sign in front of her house so that people will slow down on her street.

_____

10. A police officer arrests a person who was seen speeding away from the scene of a crime.

_____

Why Do We Need Government?

Imagine a world without any rules. It might seem fun at first, but rules and laws are necessary for a community, large or small, to run smoothly. Government can prevent people from taking advantage of others. It also works to keep order and discourage violence. Having rules and laws can make people feel more safe and secure. Government also protects people's rights and helps people who are in need.

Review the rules and laws below. Under each, write what you think would happen if the rule or law did not exist.

1. Traffic laws_____

    _____

    _____

2. Right to private property _____

    _____

    _____

3. Trial by jury_____

    _____

    _____

    _____

4. Elections of government officials _____

    _____

    _____

    _____

_____

What Does Government Do?

The government provides for many of the needs of its citizens. Its primary jobs involve making laws, carrying out laws, enforcing laws, and managing conflicts over laws. Government also provides for the defense of the nation and provides many services to people.

On the left is a list of some needs that people in a society have. On the right is a list of services that the United States government provides to meet those needs. Draw a line to connect each need with a government service. Note that more than one government service may meet the same need.

1. Education

2. Communication

3. Safety

4. Protection

5. Transportation

6. Health

7. Help for the needy

8. Clean air and water

9. Money to trade for goods

a. printing money

b. providing a police force

c. building roads

d. providing unemployment benefits

e. providing Social Security and Medicare

f. funding and staffing public schools

g. providing a military

h. setting and enforcing speed limits

i. delivering mail

j. making laws to restrict pollution

k. establishing parks and protected lands

l. establishing public libraries

m. building low-income housing

n. inspecting food and drugs

Limited vs. Unlimited Government

If government is so useful and helpful, why should we limit its power? If the leader of a country did not have to follow rules or laws, there would be no other bodies of government to check the powers of the leader. If the people of the country had no power to get rid of the leader, he could do whatever he wanted. Government would be left to the leader's ideas about how things should be run, and he would not necessarily serve the needs of the citizens. A leader could gain too much power, and there would be no way to protect the rights of individual citizens.

1. Imagine if you were the principal of your school and could run the school any way you wanted. What rules would you make? Would you make rules at all? What would school be like?

   _____

   _____

   _____

   _____

2. Think about the purpose of school. Do you think much learning would get done in your school?

   _____

   _____

3. Do you think teachers would like working for you? Do you think it would be hard to keep good teachers on your staff?

   _____

   _____

4. Do you think families would be happy with the way you ran the school?

   _____

   _____

5. How do you think families and teachers would feel if they had no way to influence your decisions and no way to remove you from your position?

   _____

   _____

Types of Government

There are many models of government in the world. Governments are classified based on who has the power and how limited or unlimited the power is. The two basic types of government are totalitarian and democratic.

In a totalitarian government, the leaders of a country have unlimited power. Totalitarian leaders often take their power by force and keep tight control over their countries and people. Types of totalitarian governments include monarchy (rule by one person of royalty), oligarchy (rule by a small, select group of people), and dictatorship (rule by one person or political party).

Democratic governments give decision-making power to the people. There are two types of democracies, direct and indirect (also called representative). In a direct democracy, the people vote on and make laws themselves. In an indirect democracy, the people elect representatives to make laws for them. Indirect democracies can be presidential or parliamentary. In a presidential system (like in the United States), the people elect a president to head the executive branch of government and members of a separate legislative branch of government to make the laws. In the parliamentary system (like in Great Britain), a political party is chosen to lead the government, and the head of that party becomes the prime minister. The prime minister is similar to a president, except that in addition to leading the executive branch, he or she also participates in the legislative branch.

Write the correct words on the lines to complete the sentences.

1. The leaders of a _____ government have unlimited power.

2. _____ governments give the power to the people.

3. Great Britain has a _____ system of indirect democracy.

4. A monarchy is ruled by one person of _____.

5. Two types of democracies are _____ and _____.

6. A government ruled by a small, select group of people is called an _____.

7. One person or political party rules a _____.

8. The leader of a parliamentary democracy is called a _____.

9. In a _____ democracy, the people make the laws themselves.

Democracy in the U.S.

The government of the United States is a democracy. The idea of democracy came from ancient Greece, where the citizens ruled the country directly. Democracy in the United States is called a republic. A republic is a representative democracy in which citizens elect other people (representatives) to make government decisions for them based on their wants and beliefs. U.S. democracy supports free elections, limits the power of government, encourages competing political parties, and protects the individual freedoms of its citizens.

Fill in the topic web below with details about U.S. democracy. Include facts from this book, from previous learning, or from new research. Also, include your opinions about U.S. democracy. Add more ovals if needed.

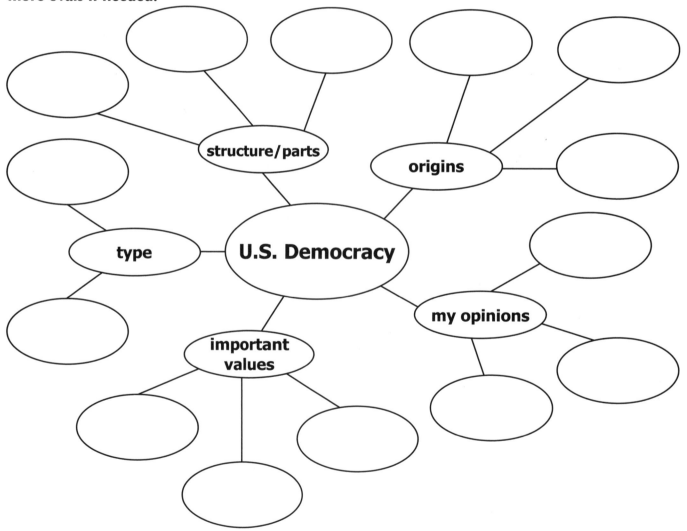

Values of American Democracy

American democracy is based on certain beliefs and values. Some of these values include justice, individual rights and freedoms (life, liberty, and the pursuit of happiness), equal opportunity, diversity, public good, patriotism, and truth.

Match each value to the correct description. Then, give a real-life example of each.

1. justice _____

   Example _____

   _____

2. individual rights and freedoms _____

   Example _____

   _____

3. equal opportunity _____

   Example _____

   _____

4. diversity _____

   Example _____

   _____

5. public good _____

   Example _____

   _____

6. patriotism _____

   Example _____

   _____

7. truth _____

   Example _____

   _____

a. qualities of life that citizens are entitled to

b. services that benefit all and help those in need

c. the honest representation of facts by government officials, media, and citizens

d. what is right and fair by the law

e. the love and support a person shows for his or her country

f. a range of customs, viewpoints, ideas, talents, and beliefs

g. the guarantee to enjoy the same rights, benefits, and choices that everyone else has

Americans' Common Beliefs

What makes an American an American? It is not because of a shared race or religion. It is not because of where an American lives or was born. What makes an American an American is his or her belief in American democracy and in other values that Americans have in common. Americans generally believe that certain things are important to their lives as Americans. These beliefs include the importance of the individual, of equality, of community (large and small), of respect for law, of education, of work, and of helping others.

Below, explain why each value is important to you and your family.

1. Individuals' rights and importance _____

_____

2. Equality _____

_____

3. Community _____

_____

4. Respect for the law _____

_____

5. Education _____

_____

6. Work _____

_____

7. Volunteering and helping others _____

_____

An American Motto

In 1776, when the Great Seal was being designed, some suggested that a familiar Latin phrase, "e pluribus unum," be used as a motto on the seal. The phrase means "out of many, one" and was probably meant to stand for the thirteen original colonies coming together to form one nation. The motto is included on the many variations of the Great Seal and also on some U.S. currency. To many Americans today, the motto represents the diversity of the country's citizens. The United States is known as a "melting pot" because its citizens come from different racial, cultural, and religious backgrounds but share common American beliefs and values.

Having people from all different races, religions, and ethnic backgrounds living together in the same country has many positive effects but can also have negative effects.

Think of the positives (pros) and negatives (cons) of a "melting pot" country and write them below.

PROS	CONS
_____	_____
_____	_____
_____	_____
_____	_____
_____	_____

Overall, do you think that living in a "melting pot" of cultures is positive or negative? Why?

_____

_____

_____

_____

Patriotism

Patriotism is the love and support that a person shows for his or her country. It is an important value to Americans although there is often disagreement about what it means to be patriotic. Patriotism is a feeling that is always present in American citizens but is more noticeable during times of national crisis, such as an act of terrorism, the assassination of a president, the declaration of war, or during American holidays, such as Independence Day, Memorial Day, and Flag Day. Many people believe that patriotism does not mean that a citizen always supports and agrees with everything the president and others in government decide. Disagreeing with and protesting the government is a basic right of U.S. citizens. A patriotic citizen is loyal to his or her country and the values and principles for which the country stands—not necessarily to the beliefs of a particular senator or president. Some Americans agree with the right to protest the government but believe that being patriotic means that citizens stand behind the government.

Write a poem about your feelings of patriotism. What makes you feel patriotic? How does it feel? What emotions are involved? How do you show your patriotism?

_____

_____

_____

_____

_____

_____

_____

_____

_____

The U.S. Flag

When the states were still colonies, they had a flag called the Grand Union Flag. It had the red and white stripes like the current U.S. flag, but the British flag was in the top left corner rather than the blue field with white stars. In 1777, a new flag was approved with 13 alternating red and white stripes and a blue field with 13 white stars. Originally, there was no particular arrangement required for the stars, which is why some flags showed the stars in a circle. This flag became known as the "Betsy Ross flag." Betsy Ross was said to have been asked by George Washington to make the first flag, but it is likely that this is not true.

When the new nation started growing, both a star and a stripe were added for each new state. It was soon realized that this could not continue, so in 1818, it was decided to leave the original 13 stripes and just add a star for each state. Today, the U.S. flag has 50 white stars.

On the lines below, write the names of the states that the stars on the U.S. flag represent. Start with the original 13 states.

1. _____
2. _____
3. _____
4. _____
5. _____
6. _____
7. _____
8. _____
9. _____
10. _____
11. _____
12. _____
13. _____
14. _____
15. _____
16. _____
17. _____
18. _____
19. _____
20. _____
21. _____
22. _____
23. _____
24. _____
25. _____

26. _____
27. _____
28. _____
29. _____
30. _____
31. _____
32. _____
33. _____
34. _____
35. _____
36. _____
37. _____
38. _____
39. _____
40. _____
41. _____
42. _____
43. _____
44. _____
45. _____
46. _____
47. _____
48. _____
49. _____
50. _____

The Pledge of Allegiance

I pledge allegiance to the flag of the United States of America and to the Republic for which it stands, one nation, under God, indivisible, with liberty and justice for all.

1. What does it mean to pledge something? _____

   _____

2. Look up the word *allegiance* in the dictionary and write the definition below.

   allegiance: _____

   _____

3. In your own words, write what it means to pledge allegiance to a flag and to the Republic for which it stands.

   _____

   _____

   _____

4. What do you think the authors of the Pledge of Allegiance meant by *indivisible*? _____

   _____

   _____

5. Why are the words *liberty* and *justice* important? What other words do you think are important to include when describing the United States? Why?

   _____

   _____

   _____

   _____

The National Anthem

The Star-Spangled Banner

Oh, say, can you see by the dawn's early light,
What so proudly we hailed at the twilight's last gleaming?

Whose broad stripes and bright stars, through the perilous fight,
O'er the ramparts we watched, were so gallantly streaming?

And the rockets' red glare, the bombs bursting in air,
Gave proof through the night that our flag was still there.

Oh, say, does that star-spangled banner yet wave
O'er the land of the free and the home of the brave?

"The Star-Spangled Banner" was written on September 14, 1814, by Francis Scott Key at Fort McHenry in Baltimore, Maryland, after a British attack in the War of 1812. Francis Scott Key went to Fort McHenry with Colonel John Skinner to ask for the release of an American prisoner, Dr. William Beanes. They sailed into the bay to meet the British fleet and get Dr. Beanes. The British gave them the prisoner but made the group stay in their boat on the water until the battle was over. At dawn, relieved to see the American flag still raised on the fort's flagpole, Key was inspired to write the poem, "The Defense of Fort McHenry." Put to the tune of a popular English song, Key's poem became known as "The Star-Spangled Banner." In 1931, the U.S. Congress voted to make "The Star-Spangled Banner" the national anthem.

Circle the letter of the best answer for each question below.

1. Who wrote the national anthem of the United States?
   a. Colonel John Skinner
   b. Francis Scott Key
   c. Dr. William Beanes

2. What was the original name of the anthem?
   a. "The Battle Flag"
   b. "The Land of the Free"
   c. "The Defense of Fort McHenry"

3. During which war was the anthem written?
   a. The War of 1812
   b. The Revolutionary War
   c. The Civil War

4. On the day after the battle, why was Key relieved to see the flag?
   a. because it meant he could go home
   b. because it meant that the fort was not captured by the British
   c. because he was worried that the flag would be stolen

The Great Seal

For many years, countries have used national seals to authenticate documents, agreements, and contracts. When the United States declared its independence from England, a committee was assigned the task of designing a seal to represent the new country. It took six years and three committees for the design of the Great Seal to be finalized and approved by Congress. The look of the seal has varied slightly over the years because the approved version is only a written description (called a blazon).

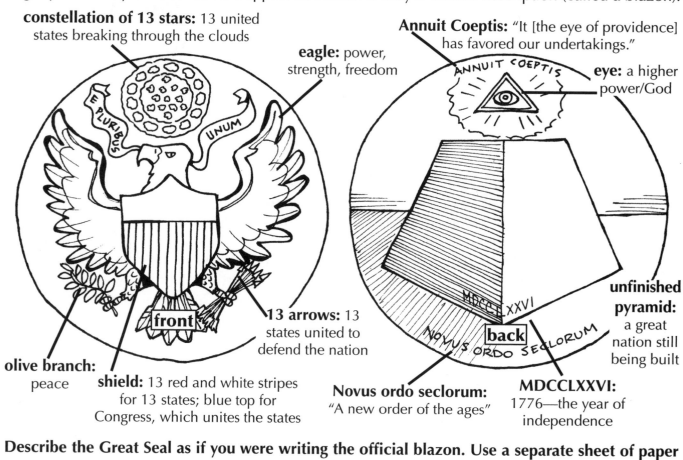

constellation of 13 stars: 13 united states breaking through the clouds

eagle: power, strength, freedom

Annuit Coeptis: "It [the eye of providence] has favored our undertakings."

eye: a higher power/God

olive branch: peace

shield: 13 red and white stripes for 13 states; blue top for Congress, which unites the states

13 arrows: 13 states united to defend the nation

Novus ordo seclorum: "A new order of the ages"

MDCCLXXVI: 1776—the year of independence

unfinished pyramid: a great nation still being built

Describe the Great Seal as if you were writing the official blazon. Use a separate sheet of paper if necessary.

_____

_____

_____

_____

_____

The Statue of Liberty

In 1884, the French gave the United States a statue—"Liberty Enlightening the World." The statue was a gift meant to celebrate the spirit of liberty and the friendship of France with the United States. Over the years, the statue has become known simply as the Statue of Liberty and has come to stand for the freedom and opportunity that the United States offers.

The Statue of Liberty is built of an iron frame and copper shell and stands in the middle of Fort Wood on Liberty Island in New York City. The statue is 151 feet and 1 inch tall and sits atop a 154-foot pedestal. The Statue of Liberty was originally designed to serve as a lighthouse, with light coming from the windows in the crown. Before the dedication in 1886, it was decided that the torch would be lit instead. But, the light from the torch ended up being too dim to see from far away. After a renovation in 1986, the torch was rebuilt and covered in gold leaf.

Because it is near the former immigration station at Ellis Island, Lady Liberty has greeted millions of immigrants who entered the United States. Many immigrants leave their countries because of harsh or unfair conditions, and the United States is a refuge for them. Poet Emma Lazarus wrote "The New Colossus," a poem about Lady Liberty welcoming these immigrants. She imagined the Statue of Liberty would say, ". . . Give me your tired, your poor, your huddled masses yearning to breathe free, the wretched refuse of your teeming shore. Send these, the homeless, tempest-tossed to me. I lift my lamp beside the golden door!" This poem is displayed on the base of the statue.

Following are some features of the Statue of Liberty and their meanings. Draw a line to match each feature with its meaning.

1. broken chain at her feet
2. crown with seven spikes
3. shining torch
4. JULY IV, MDCCLXXVI on the tablet
5. flowing robe
6. tablet in shape of a keystone

a. the light of liberty
b. book of law that holds everything together
c. seven seas and continents
d. the roman goddess of liberty
e. breaking free from tyranny (unjust rule)
f. date the Declaration of Independence was signed

The Liberty Bell

A bell was ordered from England in 1751 to celebrate the 50-year anniversary of Pennsylvania's constitution. The bell was hung in the steeple of the State House (now Independence Hall) in Philadelphia, Pennsylvania, and cracked when it was rung to test the sound. Two local foundry workers, John Pass and John Stow, melted down and recast the bell. The new bell was hung in 1753, but people didn't like its tone. Pass and Stow tried again, but the sound was still not right. Another bell was ordered from England, but it didn't sound right either, so the Pass and Stow bell stayed where it was. The bell was inscribed with a passage from the Bible, "Proclaim LIBERTY throughout all the Land unto all the Inhabitants thereof—Lev. XXV X," along with information about the origins of the bell.

The bell was rung to call meetings and to mark special events. It was also rung on July 8, 1776, to call people to come hear the first public reading of the Declaration of Independence. During the Revolutionary War, the bell was hidden in the floorboards of a church in Allentown, Pennsylvania, so that the British would not take it and melt it down for cannon shot.

There are many stories about how the Liberty Bell came to be cracked as it is today. The most common theory claims that the bell had small cracks from several events, but the large crack that left it permanently damaged happened when the bell was rung to celebrate George Washington's birthday in 1846.

The bell was first called the Liberty Bell in a poem in an antislavery pamphlet. The Liberty Bell was an important symbol for the antislavery movement. Today, the Liberty Bell resides in a glass pavilion across from Independence Hall in Philadelphia, Pennsylvania.

Answer the following questions.

1. What is a foundry? _____

2. True or False: The Liberty Bell was made in England. _____

3. Why do you think no one knows exactly when and how the Liberty Bell was cracked as it is today?

   _____

   _____

4. Why might the Liberty Bell have been an important symbol for the antislavery movement?

   _____

   _____

The Mayflower Compact

The Pilgrims were a group of people who disagreed with how the Church of England was run. They wanted to go to a place where they could establish their own church. They received permission to travel to Virginia where they could worship as they pleased. In September of 1620, about 50 Pilgrims and about 50 other Englishmen (that the Pilgrims called "Strangers") set sail for America on a ship called the *Mayflower*. In November of 1620, the ship arrived at Cape Cod in present-day Massachusetts. The water to the south was too rough and dangerous, so they decided to settle where they were.

Because the trip had not turned out as planned, some of the "Strangers" talked about leaving the group. But, the group believed they had a better chance for survival if they all stuck together, and they had a better chance of sticking together if they agreed at the start to follow certain rules. So, they wrote an agreement called the Mayflower Compact. Many people consider the Mayflower Compact to be the first form of self-government in America's history. The document declared that the group would stay together and form their own laws and government. All who signed promised to follow these laws. Forty-one men signed the compact. (Women did not have many rights at that time.) They elected John Carver as their first governor and set out to look for fresh water. After exploring the area, the travelers decided to settle nearby in Plymouth.

Circle fact or opinion for each statement below.

1. The Pilgrims' ideas about the church were better than England's ideas.   fact   opinion

2. The *Mayflower* sailed in 1620.   fact   opinion

3. Signing the Mayflower Compact was a good idea.   fact   opinion

4. Forty-one men signed the Mayflower Compact.   fact   opinion

5. John Carver was the smartest person on the *Mayflower*.   fact   opinion

6. About 100 people traveled to America on the *Mayflower*.   fact   opinion

7. The *Mayflower* did not land where the Pilgrims had first planned.   fact   opinion

8. The Mayflower Compact was a perfect agreement.   fact   opinion

Government in the Colonies

Much of the government in the colonies was based on English common law. Common law is a set of laws based on customs and the decisions of judges. Many rights in the U.S. Constitution today are based on these English common laws, including the right to vote, the right to free speech, and the right to a trial by jury.

Each colony had its own governor and two law-making groups—a council and an assembly. The system was similar to state government today, which is also usually led by a governor and two law-making groups—the senate and the house of representatives. In some colonies, these officials were elected by the people of the colonies. In other colonies, officials were chosen by the British monarchy and were responsible for making sure the colonies made money for Great Britain.

Great Britain established the colonies in America to find and control new resources. They wanted the colonists to send raw materials, such as animal skins, wood, metals, and crops, from America to Great Britain. They wanted to use the materials to make goods, like tools and clothing, to sell at high prices to the colonies and to other countries.

Imagine you are the governor of an American colony. Write a report to the King of England about your colony. Include information on what materials you send to Great Britain and how your government is running.

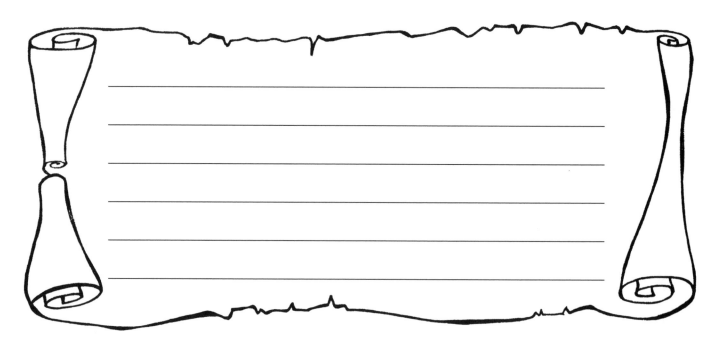

The American Revolution

Even though the colonists were still British citizens, they did not have a representative in Great Britain's government to protect their interests. The British didn't think the colonies were making enough money for them, so they put high taxes on goods and made laws that kept the American colonists from trading with other countries. This made the colonists angry. They didn't think it was fair that Great Britain could tell them what to do and make them buy expensive British goods.

Following is a list of some events that led to the American Revolution. Use the clues in the list to put the events in chronological order.

1. _____ England closed Boston Harbor until the colonists paid for the tea that they threw away.

2. _____ In 1763, the British Parliament said that the colonists could not settle west of the Appalachian Mountains.

3. _____ In 1767, the British put a tax on tea.

4. _____ After the Stamp Act was canceled, the British government made a declaration that they could make laws that the American colonies had to follow.

5. _____ The first shots of the Revolution were fired at Lexington and Concord, Massachusetts, in 1775.

6. _____ After the Sugar Act, the Stamp Act of 1765 was passed to tax all printed material, such as newspapers and licenses. It was called the Stamp Act because material had to be stamped to show that the tax was paid.

7. _____ The colonies boycotted, or refused to buy, British goods until Great Britain canceled the Stamp Act.

8. _____ In 1773, a group of colonists showed their anger over the tea tax by throwing a shipment of tea into the Boston harbor. This became known as the Boston Tea Party.

9. _____ The British passed the Sugar Act, which was a tax on non-British sugar and molasses.

Writing the Declaration of Independence

The temporary government of the United States, the Second Continental Congress, asked a group of five men to write the Declaration of Independence. The group was led by Thomas Jefferson. The other men in the group were Benjamin Franklin, John Adams, Robert Livingston, and Roger Sherman. Thomas Jefferson wrote the first draft of the declaration, and the other men edited it and made changes. It took about two weeks for the group to write the declaration. Then, the group presented the declaration to the Second Continental Congress, and they made more changes before it was officially adopted on July 4, 1776.

Answer the following questions.

1. Have you ever written a story or report that another person edited for you? _____

   _____

   _____

2. What types of changes or suggestions did he or she have for your writing? _____

   _____

   _____

   _____

   _____

3. Do you think your final draft was better after you made the changes that the person suggested?

   Why or why not? _____

   _____

   _____

4. Why do you think Thomas Jefferson had four other men edit the first draft of the Declaration of

   Independence that he wrote? _____

   _____

   _____

The Declaration of Independence

The Declaration of Independence was written after the start of the Revolutionary War to state to England and other countries that the 13 American colonies were no longer under British rule and that they were forming a new government of their own. The document was signed on July 4, 1776. Independence Day is an important holiday that is celebrated every year in the United States. Today, the original Declaration of Independence is kept in the National Archives Building in Washington, D. C.

Look at the drawing below of the Declaration of Independence. Many people signed the document, but the largest signature belongs to John Hancock. Today, to put your "John Hancock" on something means to sign your name on it. On a separate piece of paper, write a declaration of a goal you want to meet. Then, put your "John Hancock" on it and display it to inspire you to reach your goal.

Understanding the Declaration of Independence

The Declaration of Independence is organized into four main parts: the preamble, or introduction, that explains why the colonies were declaring independence; a section listing the human rights that the colonists believed in; a section listing all of the ways the British government had been mistreating the colonies; and a section declaring that the colonies were now independent states and were breaking all ties with Great Britain.

The Declaration of Independence states some important ideals of the United States. One important message in the declaration is that all people are created equal and have certain rights that should be protected, not taken away, by government. The declaration also states that government's authority should come from the people and that the people should have the right to change the government if it isn't working properly.

A famous quote from the Declaration of Independence is: *We hold these truths to be self-evident, that all men are created equal, that they are endowed by their Creator with certain unalienable Rights, that among these are Life, Liberty and the pursuit of Happiness.*

Below, write how you enjoy the rights of life, liberty, and happiness in your life and ways you think government protects you so that you can enjoy these rights.

_____

_____

_____

_____

_____

_____

_____

_____

_____

_____

_____

_____

The Articles of Confederation

Fill in the blanks with the appropriate words from the Word Bank below.

The new independent states would have to _____ together if they were going to win the _____ War against the British. The Second Continental _____ decided that they would need to assign a _____ to write a new _____ for a central government. A first _____ was written in 1777, and by 1781, all _____ states had ratified, or _____, it. The plan was called the Articles of Confederation.

The Articles of Confederation tried to set up a _____ government that still allowed each state to be _____. The national government would handle relationships with other countries, wars, the military, money, and the post office. Each state had only _____ vote and all thirteen _____ had to vote "yes" to make an _____, or change, to the Articles.

In 1787, Congress realized that a new plan of _____ was needed. The Articles of Confederation didn't give the government enough _____ to do its job. So, in 1787, a meeting was held to write a new plan—the Constitution.

Word Bank

amendment	one
approved	plan
committee	power
Congress	Revolutionary
draft	states
government	thirteen
independent	work
national	

The Constitution

The United States Constitution is a set of laws and rules that guide how the United States government is run. The Constitution explains the jobs and powers of each part of the federal government and states the basic rights of U.S. citizens.

The Constitution was designed to be flexible and change throughout the years as the needs of the citizens changed. Just like the laws of the United States, your family has rules you must live by. Describe how those rules have changed and might change in the future as you grow and change.

_____

_____

_____

_____

_____

_____

_____

_____

_____

_____

_____

_____

The Constitutional Convention

The following information contains the basic facts about the Constitutional Convention.

Pretend you were a newspaper reporter during this time and use the information to write a news article about this historic meeting.

Who: the "Founding Fathers"— 55 delegates from the 13 states; only about 35 were present during the writing of the Constitution since the meeting lasted so long and people had to come from far away; some delegates included Benjamin Franklin, James Madison, Alexander Hamilton, and George Washington, who served as president of the meeting

What: the Constitutional Convention

Where: Philadelphia, Pennsylvania

When: May 25, 1787; lasted until September of 1787

Why: to write the laws for the new government of the United States

The Constitutional Gazette

The Preamble to the Constitution

The preamble to the U.S. Constitution is a paragraph at the beginning of the Constitution that tells why the Founding Fathers wrote the Constitution. The words they used in the 1780s are very formal and can be hard to understand.

Using a dictionary, rewrite the preamble in your own words to make the message more simple and easy to understand today.

We the people of the United States, in order to form a more perfect Union, establish justice, insure domestic tranquility, provide for the common defense, promote the general welfare, and secure the blessings of liberty to ourselves and our posterity, do ordain and establish this Constitution for the United States of America.

_____

_____

_____

_____

_____

_____

_____

Government Framework

The Constitution divides the powers of the federal government into three separate branches so that one person or group cannot become too powerful. These three branches of government are called the executive branch, the legislative branch, and the judicial branch. The executive branch carries out the laws; the legislative branch makes the laws; and the judicial branch studies and makes decisions based on the laws. To help you remember which branch does what, find the verb in the dictionary that each branch is named for. Write each definition below.

1. execute: _____

_____

_____

_____

2. legislate: _____

_____

_____

_____

3. judge: _____

_____

_____

_____

_____

Checks and Balances

To prevent one branch of government from having too much power, the Constitution gives each branch the power to influence or change what another branch does. This system is called *checks and balances*. The chart below shows some of the ways that each branch can "check" another so that the government stays balanced.

Study the chart and then answer the questions.

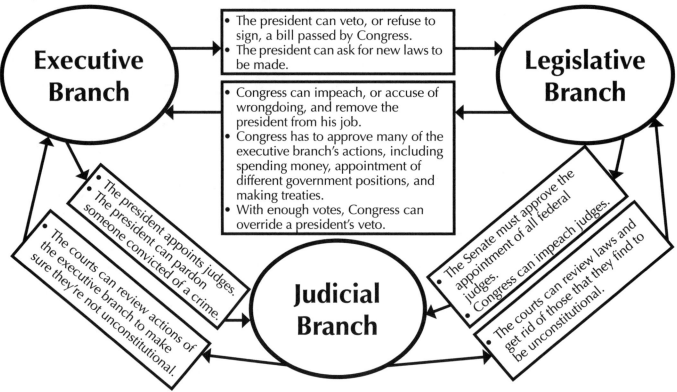

1. Which branch of government can check the judicial branch by pardoning a person convicted of a crime? _____

2. Name one way the legislative branch can check the powers of the executive branch.

   _____

3. If a law is unconstitutional, which branch of government has the power to say so and throw it out?

   _____

4. In what two ways does the president have power over which laws are made? _____

   _____

5. What part of the legislative branch checks the judicial branch by approving the appointment

   of federal judges? _____

Organization of the Constitution

The Constitution is organized into seven sections called articles. The articles are numbered using Roman numerals: I (1), II (2), III (3), IV (4), V (5), VI (6), and VII (7). After the articles is a section of amendments, or changes, to the Constitution.

Below, match each article with the correct summary of what it says. Use an encyclopedia, the Internet, or another reference to help you.

1. _____ Article I

2. _____ Article II

3. _____ Article III

4. _____ Article IV

5. _____ Article V

6. _____ Article VI

7. _____ Article VII

a. states that at least nine states must accept the Constitution before it can become law

b. states that the Constitution is the law of the land and that all senators and representatives must swear to support the Constitution

c. describes the powers of the Supreme Court and other federal courts

d. describes how the president will be elected, who can run for president, and what powers and responsibilities the president has

e. describes how to make changes to, or amend, the Constitution

f. describes how the states will relate to each other, how new states can be added to the Union, and how the federal government will protect the states

g. describes how Congress will be set up, how laws will be made, and what powers Congress will have

Ratification of the Constitution

The Constitution was signed by the delegates to the Constitutional Convention on September 17, 1787. But, the Constitution could not be made law until it was ratified, or accepted and signed, by nine of the 13 states in the Union. Eventually, all 13 states signed it.

Label the map below with the names of the states and the dates they ratified the Constitution. Lightly color the first nine states that signed. Use an encyclopedia, the Internet, or another reference to help you. (Notice that Virginia includes both present-day Virginia and West Virginia.)

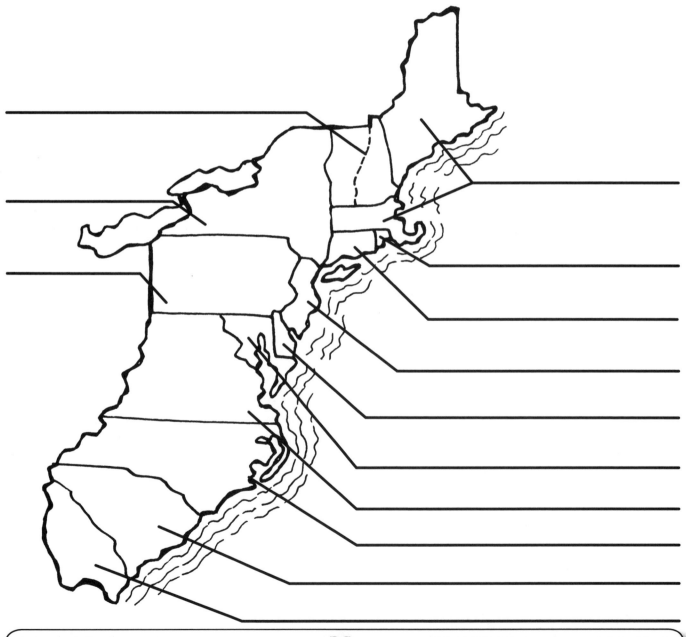

Amending the Constitution

Article V allows the Constitution to be changed and added to as the needs of the country change. These changes and additions are called *amendments*. An amendment may be proposed, or suggested, by Congress if two-thirds of the Senate and three-fourths of the House of Representatives vote for it. Then, three-fourths of the states must ratify, or approve, the amendment before it can become an official Constitutional Amendment. This process helps to make sure that only amendments that are very important and that most people agree with are accepted. Since the Constitution was written over 200 years ago, only 27 amendments have been approved.

Choose the correct answer for each question below.

1. There are 50 states, and each state is represented by two senators. At least how many senators would need to vote yes to propose an amendment to the Constitution? (Hint: You can't have a fraction of a person, so round your answer up.)

   a. 50   b. 67   c. 83   d. 75

2. If there are 435 representatives in the House of Representatives, at least how many yes votes would be needed to propose an amendment?

   a. 145   b. 200   c. 135   d. 327

3. After an amendment is proposed, how many states must ratify it before it can become a Constitutional Amendment? (Remember to round up.)

   a. 38   b. 25   c. 13   d. 40

The Bill of Rights

To convince several states to ratify the Constitution, the Founding Fathers promised to add a section of amendments that describe the basic rights and freedoms of American citizens. This section of amendments is called the Bill of Rights. These first 10 amendments to the Constitution were added in 1791.

On this page and the next, read the statements relating to each of the 10 amendments in the Bill of Rights. Then, decide whether the statements are true or false.

Amendment I
- The government cannot make a law telling you what religion to believe in.   T   F
- The government can make it illegal for you to speak your opinion.   T   F
- The government can tell the media which stories it can and cannot cover.   T   F
- Citizens can gather together in meetings as long as they are peaceful.   T   F
- A citizen can tell the government what he or she does not like and make suggestions for change.   T   F

Amendment II
Citizens can own firearms to defend themselves.   T   F

Amendment III
Citizens cannot be forced to house members of the military in their own homes. (This amendment was important to people in the 1700s but is not an issue anymore.)   T   F

Amendment IV
The government can search your home and take your things without a good reason.   T   F

Amendment V
- No one can take away your property without legal permission.   T   F
- There must be enough evidence against a person accused of a serious crime to put him or her through a trial.   T   F
- A person can be sent to court more than once for the same crime.   T   F
- Proper legal procedures have to be followed before a person can be declared guilty of a crime.   T   F
- A person can be forced to testify against himself or herself in court.   T   F

The Bill of Rights (cont.)

Amendments VI and VII

- Only certain people have the right to have a jury decide whether they are guilty or innocent.   T   F
- After a person is accused of a crime, the government can take as long as it wants to give that person a trial.   T   F
- A person cannot be sent to a trial without being told what he or she did wrong.   T   F
- A person accused of a crime can have witnesses come to court to help prove he or she is innocent.   T   F
- A person accused of a crime has the right to have a lawyer help to defend him or her in court.   T   F

Amendment VIII

- Courts cannot ask for a person to pay a bail (money that is paid to be let out of jail with the promise that the person will return for his or her trial) that is too high   T   F
- A person convicted of a crime cannot be given a punishment that is very cruel or too harsh for the crime.   T   F

Amendment IX

If a right of the citizens is not listed in the Constitution, then the government can ignore it.   T   F

Amendment X

Any power that the Constitution does not give to the federal government is given to the states and to the people.   T   F

The Civil Rights Amendments

Amendments XIII–XV are often called the civil rights amendments because they gave African-American slaves their freedom and the same rights as other Americans. The Thirteenth Amendment freed the slaves, stating that slavery was now illegal in the United States. The Fourteenth Amendment gave the freed slaves citizenship and gave them the rights and freedoms that other American citizens had. The Fifteenth Amendment gave African-Americans the right to vote, stating that all citizens (at that time, referring only to adult males) had the right to vote, regardless of their race or color. Even though these amendments were added to the Constitution, the civil rights of African-Americans still had a long way to go. It wasn't until the 1950s when Dr. Martin Luther King, Jr., Rosa Parks, and other activists began protesting unfair laws that African-Americans really began to have equal protection under the law.

Unscramble the words in the Word Bank to complete each sentence.

1. The _____ Amendment made slavery illegal in the United States.

2. The Fifteenth Amendment gave African-Americans the right to _____.

3. Only _____ citizens were allowed to vote when the Fifteenth Amendment was ratified.

4. Because of the Fourteenth Amendment, former slaves were now _____ of the United States.

5. In the 1950s, Dr. Martin Luther King, Jr. _____ laws that were unfair to African-Americans.

6. Amendments XIII–XV are sometimes called the _____ Rights Amendments.

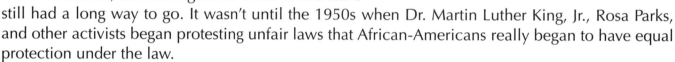

Word Bank		
eentihrTth	zceitnis	liiCv
aelm	dstorepet	teov

Women's Rights

For many years in the United States, women did not have the right to vote. In the late 1800s and early 1900s, women worked together to convince the government that they should have the right to vote. Their efforts were called the *suffrage movement*. *Suffrage* is the right to vote. In 1920, the Nineteenth Amendment was ratified. It stated that the right to vote cannot be denied based on whether a person is male or female. In the 1970s, women asked for another amendment to the Constitution that gave equal rights to women, called the ERA (Equal Rights Amendment). The ERA passed in Congress, but not enough states ratified it, so it did not become a Constitutional amendment. Some people think that the ERA is not necessary because the Fourteenth Amendment states that no *persons* who are citizens of the United States can be denied their rights.

Answer the questions below.

1. What does suffrage mean? _____

2. In what year was the Nineteenth Amendment ratified? _____

3. What right does the Nineteenth Amendment state? _____

   _____

4. What is the ERA? _____

   _____

5. Why do you think the ERA was not ratified in enough states? _____

   _____

   _____

   _____

Before the Suffrage Movement   Less Than a Century Later!

The Executive Branch

The main job of the executive branch of the U.S. government is to run the government. The executive branch is led by the president and includes many other people who help the president. Some of these people are part of the Executive Office of the President, some are part of the president's Cabinet of advisors and their departments, and others belong to the many agencies that help run government programs.

The President's Executive Office was established by President Franklin D. Roosevelt in 1939. The Executive Office includes the White House Staff and nine agencies that advise the president and provide him with information about the nation's economy, environment, security, budget, trade, and other important issues.

Fill in the missing vowels below to complete the titles of some of the offices in the White House Staff.

1. Ch___ ___ f ___f St___ff

2. Pr___ ss S___cr___t___ r y

3. sp___ ___ch wr___t___rs

4. v___s ___ t___r s ___ff___c___

5. tr___v___l ___ff___c___

6. sch___d___l___ng ___ff___c___

7. ___ff___c___ ___f c___rr___sp___nd___nc___

8. ph___t___ ___ff___c___

9. Wh___t___ H___ ___s___ c___ ___ns___l

10. the Pr___s___d___nt's phys___c___ ___n

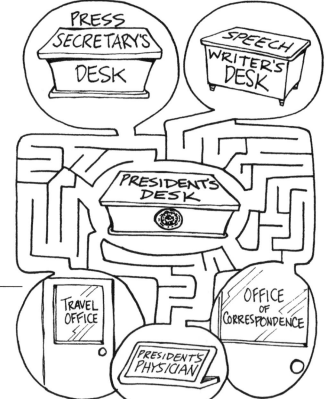

Presidential Facts

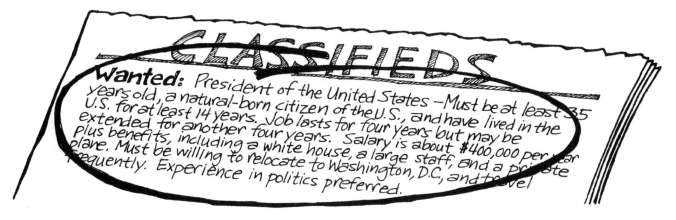

Wanted: President of the United States —Must be at least 35 years old, a natural-born citizen of the U.S., and have lived in the U.S. for at least 14 years. Job lasts for four years but may be extended for another four years. Salary is about $400,000 per year plus benefits, including a white house, a large staff, and a private plane. Must be willing to relocate to Washington, D.C., and travel frequently. Experience in politics preferred.

Read the newspaper want ad above and answer the following questions about the office of the president.

1. A person must be at least _____ years old to run for president.
   a. 44　　　　　b. 35　　　　c. 50　　　　d. 30

2. The job of president lasts for a term of _____ years.
   a. 5　　　　　b. 8　　　　c. 3　　　　d. 4

3. The president does not have to be a natural-born citizen of the U.S.
   　　　　　　true　　　　　false

4. The maximum number of full terms a person can serve as president is _____ .
   a. 2　　　　　b. 3　　　　c. 1　　　　d. 4

5. The president lives in _____.
   a. Seattle, Washington　　　　　c. Washington, D. C.
   b. Baltimore, Maryland　　　　　d. Pittsburgh, Pennsylvania

6. About how much money does the president make per year?
   a. forty thousand dollars　　　　　c. fourteen hundred dollars
   b. four million dollars　　　　　d. four hundred thousand dollars

7. A 40-year-old woman who was born in the United States, moved to France when she was six years old, and moved back to the United States when she was 26 years old can become the President of the United States.
   　　　　　　true　　　　　false

The Presidential Oath

A newly-elected president cannot start his job until he takes the oath of office at his inauguration. An inauguration is a ceremony that officially starts the beginning of a president's term of office. At noon on January 20, the Chief Justice of the Supreme Court swears in the new president. The president-elect raises his right hand, places his left hand on the Bible, and says this oath:

I do solemnly swear (or affirm) that I will faithfully execute the office of the President of the United States, and will, to the best of my ability, preserve, protect, and defend the Constitution of the United States.

The presidential oath was written in the Constitution by the Founding Fathers.

Imagine that you have to write a new oath for the President of the United States to take on Inauguration Day. Write the oath based on what you think is important for the president to promise.

_____

_____

_____

_____

_____

_____

_____

_____

President's Powers and Duties

The President of the United States has many jobs.

Match each job with the correct powers and duties.

Word Bank

| chief executive | chief of state | commander in chief of the armed forces |
| legislative leader | chief diplomat | political party leader |

---

1. _____

- makes sure federal laws are followed
- plans the national budget
- appoints federal officials, including Cabinet members, ambassadors, and Supreme Court justices
- can pardon people for crimes against the U.S.
- makes executive orders that are like laws but don't have to be approved by Congress

2. _____

- makes treaties
- talks with foreign leaders and diplomats
- proposes foreign policy

3. _____

- helps candidates from his party get elected across the country
- supports issues that are important to his party

4. _____

- appoints high-ranking military officials
- controls the size of the armed forces
- sends troops to fight but cannot declare war

5. _____

- proposes new legislation, or laws
- can veto, or refuse to sign, a bill passed by Congress
- encourages Congress to pass new laws

6. _____

- represents the United States and what it stands for to citizens and to foreign countries
- greets and hosts parties for foreign officials
- makes public appearances and performs ceremonial duties

The White House

Complete the crossword puzzle.

Across

4. The president's office is called the _____ office.
5. The White House has a swimming pool, movie theater, and _____ alley.
6. During the War of 1812, the White House was _____ down by the British.
8. The address of the White House is 1600 _____ Avenue.
10. The part of the White House where the president and his staff work each day is called the _____ Wing.

Down

1. Thomas _____ first opened the White House to public tours.
2. There are 132 _____, 35 bathrooms, and 6 floors in the White House.
3. George _____ picked the site for the White House in 1790.
7. Before the White House was burned, first lady _____ Madison saved a famous painting of George Washington.
9. John _____ was the first president to live in the White House.

Impeachment

If the president does something illegal, the House of Representatives can vote to *impeach* him. To impeach a president means to charge him with a crime. The majority of the members of the House of Representatives must vote to impeach a president before he can be impeached. Then, the Senate has a trial to decide whether the president is guilty. The Chief Justice of the Supreme Court presides over the trial, and the senators are like the jury. Two-thirds of the Senate must vote guilty for the president to be convicted. If a president is found guilty, he is removed from office and can no longer be the president. Only two presidents have ever been impeached, Andrew Johnson and Bill Clinton, but neither were convicted by Congress, and neither lost their jobs.

Match each word with the correct definition below. Use the context clues in the paragraph and a dictionary to help you.

1. impeach

    a. a group of people who decide if a person is guilty or innocent of a crime

2. illegal

    b. more than half

3. majority

    c. a job, usually in public service

4. preside

    d. to charge someone with a crime

5. convicted

    e. not allowed by law

6. jury

    f. proven guilty

7. office

    g. to be in charge; oversee

The Vice President

The vice president of the United States has a very important job. If the president gets sick or for some other reason can't do his job, the vice president fills in for him until he can work again. If the president dies or leaves the job, the vice president becomes the new president until the next election. During a normal presidency, the vice president serves as the president of the Senate. He listens to the debate but cannot participate or vote on bills. The only time the vice president can vote is in the case of a tie. Some presidents give their vice presidents additional duties and responsibilities.

Match the first and last names of former vice presidents that became presidents because of the death or resignation of the president.

1. John   a. Arthur

2. Millard   b. Truman

3. Andrew   c. Tyler

4. Chester   d. Ford

5. Theodore   e. Fillmore

6. Calvin   f. Coolidge

7. Harry   g. Johnson

8. Lyndon   h. Roosevelt

9. Gerald   i. Johnson

The Cabinet

The Cabinet is a group of 15 advisors to the president. Each advisor is the head of a special department in the executive branch. These department heads are all called Secretaries (for example, the Secretary of State is the head of the State Department), except the head of the Justice Department. Each president chooses new department heads for his Cabinet. The president's choices for his Cabinet must be approved by the Senate. The president may also ask other people to be in his Cabinet, such as the vice president, his chief of staff, and select leaders in his Executive Office.

Use the Word Bank to complete the names of each Cabinet department name. Then, write the circled letters in order to find out what the head of the Justice Department is called.

The ___ ___ ___ ___ ___ ___ ___   ___ ___ ___ ___ ___ ___ ___

1. (___) G R ___ ___ U ___ ___ ___ ___ E

2. ___ T ___ (___) E

3. ___ U S (___) ___ ___ E

4. ___ (___) M M ___ ___ C ___

5. L A ___ ___ (___)

6. T ___ ___ (___) ___ P ___ R T ___ ___ ___ ___ N

7. ___ ___ F ___ ___ S (___)

8. ___ N E ___ ___ (___)

9. H ___ ___ ___ ___ ___ N (___) & ___ R ___ ___ ___ ___ D ___ ___ ___ ___ ___ ___ ___ ___ ___ ___ ___ T

10. (___) ___ U ___ ___ ___ I O N

11. ___ (___) T ___ ___ ___ ___ O R

12. ___ (___) T ___ ___ ___ N ___ A ___ ___ ___ ___ ___ R ___

13. ___ (___) E A ___ ___ ___ Y

14. H ___ ___ ___ ___ ___ & ___ ___ M (___) ___ ___ ___ ___ V ___ ___ ___ ___ ___

15. ___ ___ ___ M ___ (___) ___ ___ ___ S ___ ___ U ___ ___ T ___

Word Bank

Housing & Urban Development
Health & Human Services
Homeland Security
Agriculture   Commerce
Justice   Interior
Defense   Education
Veterans Affairs   State
Energy
Transportation
Treasury
Labor

The Legislative Branch

The Legislative Branch of the U.S. government makes laws. It is made up of two groups: the Senate and the House of Representatives. Together, these two law-making groups are called Congress. The members of Congress are elected by the people of their states to represent them in the federal government. Congress has the power to propose amendments to the Constitution, declare war, remove a president from office, collect taxes, make regulations about the trade of goods between the states and between the U.S. and other countries, and investigate problems in the government and in the country. These are just a few of Congress's powers. The Senate and the House of Representatives each have powers of their own, too.

Decide whether each statement about the legislative branch is fact or opinion.

1. The two law-making groups of government together are called Congress.
   fact   opinion

2. The Senate is better than the House of Representatives.
   fact   opinion

3. Congress likes to propose amendments to the Constitution.
   fact   opinion

4. Members of Congress are elected by the people in their states.
   fact   opinion

5. People always elect nice congresspeople.
   fact   opinion

6. Congress has the power to remove a president from office.
   fact   opinion

7. The Legislative Branch is more important than the Executive Branch.
   fact   opinion

8. Congress can investigate a problem in the government.
   fact   opinion

9. The Senate and the House of Representatives have some of the same and some different powers.
   fact   opinion

10. Collecting taxes is a bad thing for Congress to do.
    fact   opinion

Name _____

The Great Compromise

When the Founding Fathers were writing the Constitution, there was a debate about how many representatives each state would have in the federal government. States with larger populations wanted the number of representatives to be based on the state's population. This way, larger states would have more votes in Congress than smaller states. This plan was called the Virginia Plan. States with smaller populations did not like this idea. They wanted each state to have an equal number of representatives so that small states would have as much say as large states. This plan was called the New Jersey Plan. Then, a compromise was suggested. It was called the Connecticut Plan. The Connecticut plan called for a *bicameral* legislature, or a two-house Congress. One house would have the same number of representatives from each state; this house is called the Senate. The other house would have a different number of representatives from each state, based on the state's population; this house is called the House of Representatives. The Connecticut Plan pleased both large and small states and became known as the Great Compromise.

Answer the following questions in complete sentences.

1. Why did the small states not like the Virginia Plan? _____

_____

_____

2. Why do you think the large states thought the Virginia Plan was fair? _____

_____

3. What is a compromise? _____

_____

4. Why do you think it is important for people in the government to learn to compromise?

_____

_____

5. Write about a time when you had to compromise with someone. _____

_____

_____

The Senate

The Senate is one of the two houses of the U.S. Congress, which makes the laws for the nation. There are 100 members of the Senate, or senators—two from each state. A senator must be at least 35 years old, have been a citizen of the United States for at least nine years, and be a resident of the state he or she represents. Senators serve six-year terms, and there is no limit to the number of terms they can be elected to serve. The vice president serves as the President of the Senate, but he cannot vote except to break a tie.

Because there are many bills on different topics to consider making into laws, the Senate works in committees, or small groups. Each committee has a different subject that it focuses on, such as foreign relations, transportation, or the environment. Even though committees work on their own bills, all senators vote on each bill and the majority, or more than half, must vote yes before the bill can become a law. The bill must also pass in the House of Representatives and be signed by the president before it can become a law. This is part of the Constitution's system of checks and balances.

In addition to making laws, the Senate has the power to approve the president's choices for Cabinet members, Supreme Court justices, and other federal officials. The Senate approves treaties made with other countries. The Senate also holds a trial and serves as the jury for an impeached president.

Write the missing word in each sentence below.

1. The Senate is one of the two houses of _____.

2. The Senate's main job is to make new _____ for the nation.

3. A member of the Senate is called a _____.

4. Senators serve for _____ years.

5. The President of the Senate can only vote in case of a _____.

6. Each state has _____ senators to represent them.

7. Senators work in groups called _____.

8. The _____ of senators must vote yes on a bill before it can become a law.

9. The Senate must _____ the president's choices for his Cabinet.

The House of Representatives

The House of Representatives is one of the two houses of the U.S. Congress, which makes the laws for the nation. There are 435 members of the House of Representatives. The number of representatives from each state is figured by comparing the population in that state to the total population of the country. Each state is guaranteed at least one representative. A representative must be at least 25 years old, have been a citizen of the United States for at least seven years, and live in the state he or she represents. Representatives serve two-year terms, and there is no limit to the number of terms that they can be elected to serve.

The leader of the House of Representatives is called the Speaker of the House. The Speaker can vote on a bill but usually does not, unless it is to break a tie. The House of Representatives works in committees on different topics just like the Senate. Also like the Senate, a majority vote is needed to pass a bill. In addition to law-making, the House of Representatives has the power to impeach a president.

Use the Internet to find the number of representatives each state currently has. A good Web site to try is the House of Representatives's Web site: www.house.gov.

Alabama: _____
Alaska: _____
Arizona: _____
Arkansas: _____
California: _____
Colorado: _____
Connecticut: _____
Delaware: _____
Florida: _____
Georgia: _____
Hawaii: _____
Idaho: _____
Illinois: _____
Indiana: _____
Iowa: _____
Kansas: _____
Kentucky: _____

Louisiana: _____
Maine: _____
Maryland: _____
Massachusetts: _____
Michigan: _____
Minnesota: _____
Mississippi: _____
Missouri: _____
Montana: _____
Nebraska: _____
Nevada: _____
New Hampshire: _____
New Jersey: _____
New Mexico: _____
New York: _____
North Carolina: _____
North Dakota: _____

Ohio: _____
Oklahoma: _____
Oregon: _____
Pennsylvania: _____
Rhode Island: _____
South Carolina: _____
South Dakota: _____
Tennessee: _____
Texas: _____
Utah: _____
Vermont: _____
Virginia: _____
Washington: _____
West Virginia: _____
Wisconsin: _____
Wyoming: _____

The Capitol Building

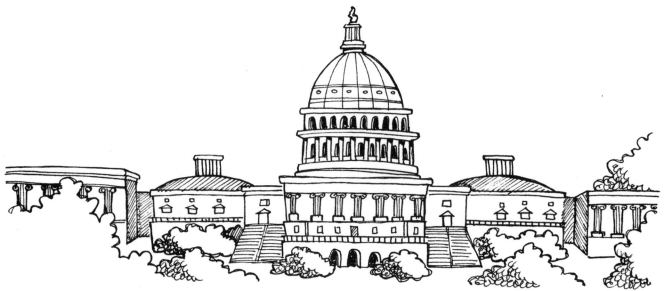

Fill in the blanks to complete the paragraph about the U.S. Capitol. If necessary, use the Internet for help.

The Capitol building in _____ , D. C., is where both houses

of Congress meet to debate and vote on new _____. The Capitol

was designed by William Thornton and sits in an area of Washington called

_____ Hill. Congress first met in the Capitol in 1800.

The Capitol is a large, white building with a huge iron _____ in the

center. On top of the dome is a bronze _____ of a woman who

represents freedom. The Senate chambers, or rooms, are in the _____

wing of the building and the _____ chambers are in the south

wing. New presidents are traditionally _____ , or sworn into office,

on the Capitol steps.

 CD-104323 U.S. Government and Presidents

How Laws Are Made

Following are the basic steps for how a law is made:

1. A bill, the first draft of a law, is introduced by a member of Congress.
2. The bill is studied by a committee.
3. The committee decides whether the bill would make a good law or whether it should be tabled, or set aside, because it would not make a good law.
4. The bill is discussed by the entire House of Representatives or entire Senate, depending on which house introduced the bill.
5. The House or the Senate votes on the bill.
6. If a bill passes in the House, it goes to the Senate for approval. If the bill passes in the Senate first, it goes to the House for approval.
7. If both the House and the Senate agree that the bill would make a good law, but disagree about certain parts of the bill, a joint committee, made up of members of both the House and the Senate, will work to make the bill acceptable to both houses.
8. If both houses of Congress pass the bill, it is sent to the president to sign.
9. If the president signs the bill, it becomes a law.
10. If the president vetoes, or does not sign, the bill, it goes back to Congress. If Congress still thinks the bill should become a law, they can override the president's veto. To override a presidential veto, at least two-thirds of the Senate and two-thirds of the House of Representatives must vote yes.

Answer the following questions.

1. What is a bill? _____

2. What happens after a bill is introduced by a member of Congress? _____

_____

3. What does it mean to table a bill? _____

_____

4. True or False: A bill can be sent to the president to sign if only one house of Congress passes it.

_____

5. True or False: A bill cannot become a law if the president does not sign it. _____

6. Both the president's veto and Congress's power to override the president's veto are examples of what important feature of the U.S. government?

_____ and _____

What Makes a Good Law?

When senators and representatives study a bill to decide if it would make a good law, they first need to decide whether there is a need for the law. They also make sure that the law promotes the common good, or does something good for the people. A law is often many pages long, so it needs to be written clearly. It should be easy to understand the purpose of the law and how it will work. A law cannot ask for things that aren't possible or practical, like a big screen television for every family in America. A law cannot go against something that the Constitution says is legal or illegal, and it cannot hurt people or take away people's rights.

Below, write a "bill" for a "law" that you would like to see made into a classroom rule. Then, below your bill, explain how it meets the qualities of a good law.

_____

_____

_____

_____

_____

_____

_____

_____

_____

The Judicial Branch

The Judicial Branch of the U.S. Government studies the laws and makes decisions about what laws mean and how laws should be followed in different situations. They also make sure that the laws in the Constitution are not broken and that people's rights and freedoms are protected.

The judicial branch is made up of the Supreme Court and other federal courts. Federal courts hear cases that deal with federal laws, the U.S. government, laws and actions that might be unconstitutional, conflicts between the states or between the U.S. and other countries, and bankruptcy. Federal judges are appointed by the president, and there is no limit to how long they can serve. Only Congress can remove a federal judge from his or her job, using the same impeachment power they have to remove the president from office.

You be the judge. Read the situation and the related classroom rules below. Decide how to settle the problem and explain why you made that decision based on the classroom rules.

Karin traded her sparkle pencil for Deshana's doodle pen. Karin broke Deshana's pen and wants her pencil back. Deshana is mad that Karin broke her pen, and wants to keep Karin's pencil and wants Karin's eraser, too. The classroom rules are: 1. no trading and 2. If you break or lose someone's property, you must replace it or give them something of equal value.

_____

_____

_____

_____

_____

_____

_____

_____

_____

Trials and Appeals

There are two basic types of trials, civil trials and criminal trials. A civil trial settles a disagreement between two people or groups. A criminal trial decides if a person or group is guilty of breaking a law. In either type of trial, the defendant, the person or group being brought to trial, has the right to be judged by a jury. A jury is a group of 12 citizens, chosen at random, who listen to the witnesses and evidence and decide the outcome of the trial. A judge makes sure that the trial runs according to the law, and lawyers use the law and the evidence to convince the jury to vote a certain way.

If a person is found guilty and thinks the trial was unfair, he or she can appeal the case. An appeal means to ask for another trial in a higher court in hopes that the verdict will be changed from guilty to not guilty. Higher courts are called courts of appeals, and the highest court in the United States is called the Supreme Court.

Write words from the paragraphs above for the definitions below. The words will sound like the words shown in parentheses.

1. A person on trial (amendment) _____

2. Twelve citizens asked to judge a trial (fury) _____

3. Type of trial that settles a disagreement (nibble) _____

4. People at a trial who tell what they saw or know (hit misses) _____

5. Information gathered that relates to a crime (mend a fence) _____

6. To take your case to a higher court (a wheel) _____

7. The decision in a trial (fur picked) _____

8. An event in a court to settle an argument or decide if someone has broken the law (mile)

   _____

9. The person who runs the trial (fudge) _____

The U.S. Supreme Court

The U.S. Supreme Court is the highest court in the country. Its main job is to rule on cases that involve questions about laws in the Constitution. The Supreme Court also has the last say in cases that have been through lower courts. The Supreme Court is not like a trial court. Instead of one judge, there are nine, and there is no jury of U.S. citizens to make the decisions. The judges make the final decisions, called rulings. The Supreme Court cannot make new laws, but their rulings are similar to laws because all other courts must follow their decisions.

The judges on the U.S. Supreme Court are called justices. Supreme Court justices are chosen by the President of the United States with approval from the Senate. After a judge is chosen as a Supreme Court justice, he or she has the job for life.

Circle yes or no for each question.

1. Can another court change the decision of a Supreme Court case?

   yes   no

2. Does the Supreme Court use a jury to make decisions?

   yes   no

3. Do other courts have to follow Supreme Court rulings?

   yes   no

4. Is there more than one judge in the Supreme Court?

   yes   no

5. Does the U.S. Senate choose the Supreme Court justices?

   yes   no

6. Does a Supreme Court justice lose his or her job after 10 years?

   yes   no

7. Can the Supreme Court write new laws?

   yes   no

8. Does the Supreme Court settle questions about the Constitution?

   yes   no

A Federal Government

The United States is called a federal government because the power is shared between the central government and the state and local governments. In the United States, each state can make its own laws for its citizens, but all citizens must follow the national laws, too. The central government has enough power to keep the states united as a country, but not so much power that states and cities can't make laws to meet their needs.

Look at the list of government powers in the box below. Decide whether the state government, the federal government, or both governments have each power. Write them in the correct parts of the Venn diagram.

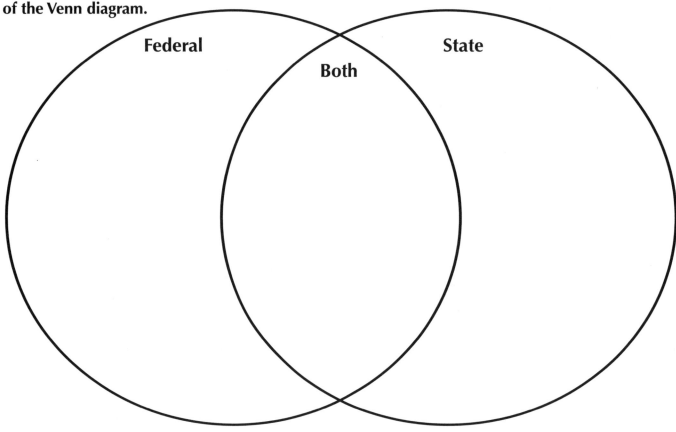

declare war	print money
enforce laws	establish public schools
run elections	take land to make parks
build roads	establish armed forces
give licenses to doctors, lawyers, and teachers	collect taxes
make treaties with other countries	establish courts
ratify Constitutional amendments	establish post offices
give marriage licenses	borrow money

Name _____

State Government

From Alaska to Hawaii and California to Maine, the states of the United States are so different and have such different concerns that federal laws cannot meet each state's specific needs. State government allows each state to make rules and laws that are specific to its state. Each state has a capital city, like the country's capital, Washington, D. C., where the government does its work. The organization of state government is very similar to the organization of the federal government. Each state in the United States has an executive, legislative, and judicial branch of government. The executive branch in state government is headed by the state's governor. The legislative branch in most state governments has an upper house (usually called a senate) and a lower house (usually called a house of representatives, but sometimes called by other names) to make laws. The judicial branch in state government contains state courts and a state supreme court. Each state also has its own constitution. A state's constitution and laws can be very different from another's, but cannot go against the U.S. Constitution.

Circle true or false for each statement below.

1. Each state's constitution is the same.   true   false

2. Each state has three branches of government.   true   false

3. Every state has two houses in the legislative branch.   true   false

4. Every state has a governor.   true   false

5. A state's constitution can keep women from voting in that state.   true   false

6. A governor is to a state as the president is to the country.   true   false

7. State governments do their work in Washington, D. C.   true   false

8. Federal laws are not specific enough to meet all state's needs.   true   false

9. Each state has a supreme court.   true   false

10. The executive branch makes the laws in state government.   true   false

Your Government

Research to find out who represents you in your state government and in the federal government. Because each state is different, you may not be able to answer all of the questions.

1. What is your state's capital city? _____

2. Who is your state's governor? _____

3. Who is your state's lieutenant governor? (A lieutenant governor is like the governor's vice president.)

   _____

4. Who is the speaker of the house in your state house of representatives?

   _____

5. Who represents you in your state senate (upper house)? _____

6. Who represents you in your state house (lower house)? _____

7. Who represents you in the U.S. Senate? _____

   _____

8. Who represents you in the U.S. House of Representatives? (often called your congressperson)

   _____

9. Who are the justices in your state's supreme court?

   _____

   _____

   _____

   _____

   _____

Making State Laws

Your state lawmakers and governor work to educate you and keep you safe and healthy. Making laws in state government is similar to making laws in the federal government, even though each state may do things differently. State senators and representatives suggest new laws, work in committees to decide if they are good laws or not, and vote on whether to pass the laws. The governor, like the president, can help make suggestions for new laws and has the power to veto a proposed law. Some states allow their citizens to vote directly on new laws. Sometimes laws are suggested by citizens who write letters to their state representatives.

Write a letter to one of your state officials. You may want to tell him or her about a problem in your neighborhood, suggest a new law, or just say thank you for a job well done. Write your final draft on good paper and send your letter.

_____ ,

_____

_____

_____

_____

_____

_____

_____

_____

_____

_____

_____ ,

_____

Local Government

Most states are divided into sections called *counties*, and each county has its own government. Within each county there are cities and towns, and each city and town has a government. These local governments often take care of the health, welfare, and education of their citizens, and manage local transportation and public utilities, such as water and electricity. They also protect their citizens with sheriff's offices, police forces, and fire departments. Local government is organized differently in each state. Most counties are governed by groups of people elected by the citizens. Most cities and towns are also governed by groups of people elected by the citizens, including mayors. A mayor's job for a city is like a governor's job for a state and the president's job for the country. Do you know who the mayor of your city or town is?

Choose the best answer for each question.

1. The sections that states are divided into are usually called
   _____.
   a. towns   b. countries   c. governments   d. counties

2. What do local governments take care of for their citizens?
   a. health   b. education   c. safety   d. all of the above

3. Which of the following is a public utility?
   a. water   b. gasoline   c. grass   d. lightbulbs

4. What group works to protect citizens?
   a. police force   b. fire department   c. sheriff's office   d. all of the above

5. Most cities and towns have a _____.
   a. president   b. mayor   c. governor   d. skyscraper

6. A city's mayor is like a state's _____.
   a. president   b. county   c. governor   d. sheriff

7. Most counties are run by groups that are _____ by the citizens.
   a. liked   b. managed   c. elected   d. hired

Taxes

The local, state, and federal governments do many things for the citizens of the United States, but they can't do it for free. The government needs money to build schools, print money, and help needy citizens. It also must have money to pay the salaries of the people who work for the government. So, where does it get this money? Much of it comes from U.S. citizens in the form of taxes. A tax is money paid to the government by businesses and individual people. Three common types of taxes are income tax, property tax, and sales tax.

Everyone in the U.S. who earns more than a certain amount of money each year must pay a percentage, or part, of that money to the government in taxes. Income taxes are due each year on April 15. Most people estimate, or guess, how much they will owe and pay their taxes a little each month so that they will not owe so much at once. Sometimes people estimate too much tax for the year. Those people get refunds from the government for the amount paid over what was owed. Sometimes people estimate too little tax and owe more money. Income tax usually helps to pay for federal and state government to function.

Property tax is a tax mostly on cars, land, houses, and other buildings. The tax is a percentage of the value of property, such as a house or car. Property tax usually pays for local government.

Sales tax is a tax on goods and services people buy. The tax is a percentage of the cost of an item. Sales tax usually pays for state government. Some states do not tax things that are necessary for daily life, such as food, clothing, and medicine. Some states put higher taxes on things that are not necessary, such as cigarettes or alcohol. Some states do not have sales tax at all.

Some people think taxes are unfair. They do not want to give the government money that they earned. What do you think?

Below, explain why you think taxes are fair or unfair. If you think they are unfair, suggest another way for the government to get money to pay for all that it does.

_____

_____

_____

_____

_____

What Do Taxes Pay For?

Unscramble the following things that government pays for with taxes. Then, write the circled letters in order to see the name of a special tax that provides money for elderly and disabled citizens.

1. OPSTLA EEVRICS   __ __ __ __ __ ⃝ __ __

2. HCSSOLO   __ __ ⃝ __ __ __

3. RACEMIDE   __ __ __ ⃝ __ __ __

4. EARRILBSI   ⃝ __ __ __ __ __ __

5. DAROS   __ ⃝ __ __

6. FREWALE   __ __ ⃝ __ __ __

7. CTUROS   __ __ __ __ ⃝

8. COLIPE   __ __ __ __ __ ⃝

9. ADERM ORCEFS   __ __ __ __ __   __ ⃝ __ __

10. CLUBIP GOUHNIS   __ __ __ __ __ __   __ __ ⃝ __ __ __

11. SONRIPS   __ ⃝ __ __ __ __ __

12. INIFTSECCI CHARESER   __ __ ⃝ __ __ __ __ __ __ __

__ __ __ __ __ __ __ __ __

13. NIOTALAN BETD   __ __ __ __ __ __ __   __ __ __ ⃝

14. UMPELONEMNTY   __ __ __ __ __ __ ⃝ __ __ __ __

15. ___ ___ __ __ __ __ __ __   __ __ __ __ __ __ __ __

Budgeting

The federal government gets its money from taxes and has to decide how it will spend it all. There are many things to pay for, and it is hard to decide how much to spend on each thing. Often, the government wants to do more than it has the money to pay for, so it borrows money. This borrowed money becomes what is called the national debt. Below is a list of things you might want to buy or do that cost money. Each item has a range of money you could spend for it. The more money you spend, the better product or service you get. (Consumer note: This is not always true, but for this activity, pretend it is.) You have only $50 to spend, but you want to do as much as you can with it. You have extra money in your savings account, and your brother said that you can borrow some from him, too.

You must decide which things you will buy and how much you will spend on each. Try not to borrow from your savings or your brother—you will go into debt! Circle your choices and write how much you chose to spend on each. Show your math to get your total spent, and then explain why you chose to buy the things you did.

birthday gift for Mom ($10-$25) _____   helmet & pads for scooter ($15–$20) _____

cellular phone ($0–$40) _____   book ($7–$16) _____

cellular phone service ($25–$38) _____   guitar ($31–$50) _____

video game ($15–$33) _____   guitar lessons ($5–$9) _____

new shoes ($29–$50) _____   pizza ($6–$12) _____

scooter ($22–$48) _____   movie ticket ($2–$8) _____

_____

_____

_____

_____

_____

_____

Voting in the U.S.

In the Gettysburg Address, Abraham Lincoln said that the U.S. government is a "government of the people, by the people, and for the people." To be a government by the people, or a democracy, there must be ways for citizens to participate in government. One main way U.S. citizens participate in government is by voting. Amendment XXVI of the U.S. Constitution gives all citizens age 18 and older the right to vote. When a citizen turns 18, he or she registers to vote, which officially puts his or her name on the list of voters. Then, when that citizen votes, the name is crossed off the list to make sure each person only gets one vote. Voting is done by secret ballot. A ballot is a list of candidates on which a person marks his or her vote. A secret ballot makes sure that each citizen's vote is private, so a citizen can vote without worrying about what other people think. The way citizens vote is different from state to state and town to town. Some common ways to vote include a punch card, a machine with pull-down levers, and a touch-screen computer. Most voting takes place on Election Day. Election Day is the first Tuesday after the first Monday in November. A presidential election is held every four years. New senators, congresspeople, and state and local officials are elected when their terms are up.

Answer the following questions.

1. Do you think voting results would be different if voting was not done by a secret ballot? Why or why not?

   _____

   _____

   _____

   _____

2. Do you think voting is an important thing for citizens to do? Why or why not?

   _____

   _____

   _____

   _____

The Electoral College

When writing the U.S. Constitution, the Founding Fathers set up a special way for the president to be elected. The president is officially elected by the Electoral College. This college is not a school; it is a group of people from each state called *electors* who vote to elect the new president. This is the basic procedure for electing a president:

1. Each political party chooses a group of electors in each state. These electors promise to vote for their party's presidential candidate. The number of electors each state gets is equal to the total number of representatives and senators they have in Congress.
2. On Election Day, citizens do not vote directly for the president. They vote for the group of electors who have promised to vote for the candidate they want to be the new president.
3. The electors who get the most votes represent the state in the Electoral College vote.
4. In December, the electors from each state vote for the president.
5. The candidate who wins the majority, or more than half, of the electoral votes is the new president.

The number of votes each candidate's electors get is called the popular vote. Sometimes a candidate can win the popular vote but still lose the election because he did not get enough electoral votes.

Below is a map of the U.S. Each state is marked with its abbreviation. Use the Internet to find the number of electoral votes for each state. Write the number on each state or in the blank provided.

1. How many electoral votes are needed for a candidate to win a presidential election?

_____

2. Which states do you think are the most important to win? Why?

_____

The Political Parties

Most U.S. citizens belong to a political party, or group that shares the same ideas about government. Political parties try to get people from their party elected to government so that their ideas can be put into action. There are two main political parties in the United States: the Democratic Party and the Republican Party.

The Democratic Party generally believes that the federal government should take care of needy citizens. Democrats usually want to raise taxes so that they can pay for government programs to help people. Overall, Democrats think that more federal government control of things is better.

The Republican Party generally believes that state government and local government should be able to take responsibility for their citizens. Republicans usually want to lower taxes and reduce the number of federal government programs. Overall, Republicans think that less federal government control of things is better.

There are several smaller political parties, called third parties or minority parties, that have come and gone throughout the years. Today, some of those parties are the Green Party, the Reform Party, the Libertarian Party, and the Independent Party. These "third" parties usually do not have enough supporters or money to get candidates elected to the presidency.

Write the correct word in each sentence below.

1. A political party is a group of citizens with the same _____ about government.

2. There are _____ main political parties in the U.S.

3. The _____ Party generally believes that less federal government control is better.

4. The _____ Party generally believes that more federal government control is better.

5. Democrats usually want to _____ taxes.

6. Republicans usually want to _____ taxes.

7. Republicans believe that more power should be given to _____ governments.

8. Democrats believe that the federal government should pay to take care of _____ citizens.

Party Symbols

Each party has an animal symbol that has come to represent it. These animals gradually became symbols for the political parties because of their use in political cartoons.

Complete the chart below by finding common facts, generalizations, and/or stereotypes about each party. An example has been provided.

The Democratic Party	The Republican Party
• prefers a strong federal government	• prefers giving states more power
• _____	• _____
• _____	• _____
• _____	• _____
• _____	• _____
• _____	• _____
• _____	• _____
• _____	• _____
• _____	• _____
• _____	• _____
• _____	• _____

The Campaign Trail

When a person wants to be elected as a government official, he or she must run a political campaign. A campaign is an organized effort to get people to vote for a particular candidate. Before campaigning, a candidate must have a platform. A platform is a written statement describing what the candidate thinks about different political issues and what he or she plans to do if elected. Next, the candidate asks the people in his or her party to donate money to help pay for the campaign. This is called fund-raising. A political campaign can be very expensive, especially a presidential campaign. The candidate has to pay people to help with the campaign. A candidate also must advertise and travel across the state or country to get his or her name and message out to people so that they will want to vote for him or her.

Many people may want to run for the same job, so there is an election in the spring called a primary election to choose one candidate from each political party to run for each office in the general election in the fall. For presidential candidates, there is a national convention for each political party. At the convention, people from each state, called delegates, vote to choose which candidate will run in the general election. The candidates who are chosen continue their campaigns by meeting and talking to more people around the country, making speeches about their platforms, and having debates with the other candidates.

Match the following words with the correct definitions.

1. An organized effort to get people to vote for a particular candidate.

2. A written statement describing what the candidate thinks about political issues and what he or she plans to do in office.

3. Asking people to donate money to pay for a political campaign.

4. A type of election to choose one candidate from each party to run in the general election.

5. People from each state who vote for a presidential candidate at their party's national convention.

6. A person running in an election.

a. primary

b. candidate

c. campaign

d. delegates

e. platform

f. fund-raising

Choosing Responsible Leaders

It is important for the people who run the government to be strong leaders. They also should have certain personal qualities and character traits.

Read the Word List of qualities that citizens should look for when choosing a government leader. Then, find the words that appear in capital letters in the word list.

Word List

HONEST
COOPERATES with others
INTELLIGENT
WORKS hard
PATRIOTIC
RESPONSIBLE
COMPASSIONATE
COMMUNICATES well

RESPECTS citizens' rights
DEPENDABLE
FAIR
COURAGEOUS
is a good CITIZEN
PERSEVERES
has VALUES and PRINCIPLES
good DECISION maker

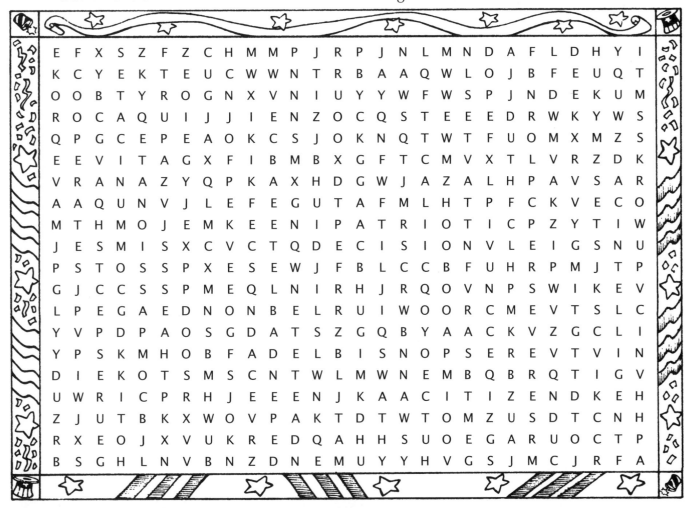

Citizenship

1. What does being a citizen of a country mean to you?

   _____

   _____

   _____

   _____

2. To be a citizen of the United States, a person must have been born in the United States, have been born to American parents in another country, or have taken a test to become a citizen. Citizens of the United States are given certain rights, including those rights stated in the Constitution, and equal protection under the law.

   What are some rights that citizens are guaranteed under the Constitution?

   _____

   _____

   _____

   _____

3. In return for the rights and privileges of U.S. citizenship, citizens must promise to follow the laws.

   What are some U.S. laws that citizens must follow?

   _____

   _____

   _____

   _____

   _____

Naturalization

Many people move to the United States each year. Just because a person now lives in the U.S. does not mean he or she automatically becomes a U.S. citizen. A person who *immigrates* (or leaves his or her country to go live in another country) to the U.S. must have a green card, or permission from the government, to stay. After a person has a green card, he or she is called a resident alien. In this case, alien means someone from another country—not from another planet! Resident aliens can own property, work, and go to school, just like citizens. They must follow the laws of the U.S. and pay taxes, just like citizens, but they cannot vote or be elected to a government office. A resident alien may become a citizen of the United States through a process called naturalization. To become naturalized, a person must take a test to show that he or she can read, speak, and write basic English and knows about U.S. laws and history. If a person passes the test, he or she will take an oath promising loyalty to the U.S., and then he or she is a U.S. citizen. The only thing a naturalized citizen cannot do that most other citizens can is become the president or vice president of the United States.

On a separate sheet of paper, answer these questions. They are similar to those found on the U.S. citizenship test.

1. What do the stars on the flag stand for?

2. Why do Americans celebrate the 4th of July?

3. What is the highest law in the United States called?

4. Which branch of government makes the laws?

5. Who wrote most of the Declaration of Independence?

6. What is the highest court in the United States?

7. What is the capital of your state?

8. In which part of the Constitution is the freedom of speech described?

9. What was the name of the ship that brought the Pilgrims to America?

10. What is a change to the Constitution called?

11. What are the two main political parties in the U.S.?

12. What is the name of the house where the president lives?

13. What nation did America fight in the Revolutionary War?

Citizens' Rights

A citizen of the United States has many rights and freedoms that cannot be taken away as long as he or she does not break the law. U.S. citizens have the right to:

- live where they want
- be friends with whomever they want
- travel freely in and out of the country
- say whatever they want as long as it is not a lie meant to hurt someone
- meet with other people to talk about whatever they want
- practice any religion they want
- criticize the government
- run for a position in government
- own property
- work where they want
- start their own businesses
- be treated the same as everyone else
- vote
- leave the U.S. to live in another country

Look at the list of freedoms above. Which ones are the most important to you? Why?

_____

_____

_____

_____

_____

_____

_____

_____

Citizens' Responsibilities

With rights come responsibilities. For example, maybe your family lets you stay up late to watch a movie, but then you are responsible for getting up in the morning to go to school; or your friend lets you borrow his video game, but you are responsible for not losing or breaking it and for returning it on time. U.S. citizens have responsibilities, too. Each citizen must obey the law, respect the rights of others, pay taxes, and serve on a jury or in the military if called to. There are also personal responsibilities that are not required by the law but are expected of a good citizen. These responsibilities include taking care of yourself and your family, helping others, accepting responsibility for your own actions, going to school, working at a job, and voting.

Answer the following questions.

1. What are some responsibilities that the law requires of U.S. citizens?

   _____

   _____

   _____

   _____

2. Why do you think it is important for citizens to go to school?

   _____

   _____

   _____

   _____

3. What are some ways that you can be a good citizen?

   _____

   _____

   _____

   _____

What Can You Do?

One of the biggest responsibilities a citizen has is to participate in government. You do not need to run for mayor or senator to participate. When you are 18, voting is one of the most important things you can do to participate in government. Right now, though, you can talk with friends and family about community issues, write to government officials with concerns and suggestions, write to newspapers or television stations with your opinions, volunteer for community organizations, and learn about what is going on in your community, state, country, and world.

Choose an issue you believe in or a problem you think the government (federal, state, or local) should do something about. Then, draw a poster about your message.

U.S. Presidents

There have been 44 U.S. presidents since 1789. Some served one term, some served two terms, some were vice presidents who finished a term when the president died, and some were even related to each other.

Work with a partner to see how many U.S. presidents you can name.

1. _____
2. _____
3. _____
4. _____
5. _____
6. _____
7. _____
8. _____
9. _____
10. _____
11. _____
12. _____
13. _____
14. _____
15. _____
16. _____
17. _____
18. _____
19. _____
20. _____
21. _____
22. _____

23. _____
24. _____
25. _____
26. _____
27. _____
28. _____
29. _____
30. _____
31. _____
32. _____
33. _____
34. _____
35. _____
36. _____
37. _____
38. _____
39. _____
40. _____
41. _____
42. _____
43. _____
44. _____

George Washington

1st President
Born: February 22, 1732 in Westmoreland County, Virginia
Political Party: Federalist
Term of Office: two terms from April 30, 1789 to March 3, 1797
Vice President: John Adams
Died: December 14, 1799

George Washington had many jobs before becoming the first president of the United States. He had been a surveyor, a farmer at his Virginia home of Mount Vernon, a member of Virginia government, a military leader during the French and Indian War, commander in chief of the army during the Revolutionary War, a delegate to the Continental Congress, and chairman of the Constitutional Convention. George Washington is called the Father of His Country and was the first signer of the Constitution. He was admired and respected and was the only president to be elected by a *unanimous* (all in agreement) vote. He was also the only president who never lived in the White House. George Washington married a *widow* (a woman whose husband has died) named Martha Custis. She had two children, but Washington never had any children of his own. There are many stories about George Washington, and some of the most famous are not true. Washington did wear false teeth, but they were not made of wood. He did not wear a wig, and he did not chop down his father's cherry tree as a child. When he died, he was remembered as being "first in war, first in peace, and first in the hearts of his countrymen."

In the story about Washington chopping down the cherry tree, George told his father that he could not tell a lie.

Rewrite each of the following sentences that George could have said about himself so that he does not tell a lie.

1. Before I became president, I worked as a lawyer.

   _____

2. I was the third president of the United States.

   _____

3. The name of my home was Monticello.

   _____

4. I was the commander in chief of the army during the Civil War.

   _____

John Adams

2nd President
Born: October 30, 1735 in Braintree, Massachusetts
Political Party: Federalist
Term of Office: one term from March 4, 1797 to March 3, 1801
Vice President: Thomas Jefferson
Died: July 4, 1826

John Adams graduated from Harvard and worked in Massachusetts as a lawyer. Adams was a strong supporter of independence from Great Britain. He did not like the way the British treated the American colonies. As a delegate to the Continental Congress, he was asked to help write the Declaration of Independence. During the Revolutionary War, Adams served as a diplomat in Europe. In 1764, Adams married an educated woman named Abigail Smith. John and Abigail had five children. Their oldest son, John Quincy, became the sixth president. Abigail talked with her husband about political matters and was a supporter of women's rights. In 1789, John Adams became Washington's vice president. During his own presidency, Adams often quarreled with his vice president, Thomas Jefferson. They disagreed about many political decisions. Adams is remembered for helping to write the treaty that ended the Revolutionary War and for keeping the United States from going to war with France.

Complete the crossword puzzle.

Across
4. John married _____ in 1764.
6. Abigail Adams believed in women's _____.
7. Adams helped to write the Declaration of
   _____.
8. Adams belonged to the _____ party.

Down
1. Adams helped to write the _____ that ended the Revolutionary War.
2. Adams's son, John _____, became the sixth president.
3. Adams was a _____ in Europe.
5. Adams kept the U.S. from going to war with _____.

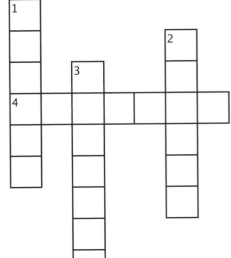

Name _____

Thomas Jefferson

3rd President
Born: April 13, 1743 in Goochland County, Virginia
Political Party: Democratic-Republican
Term of Office: two terms from March 4, 1801 to March 3, 1809
Vice Presidents: Aaron Burr (first term) and George Clinton (second term)
Died: July 4, 1826

Thomas Jefferson was an intelligent and well-educated man. He studied many subjects at the College of William and Mary, including science, math, language, philosophy, and law. Thomas Jefferson was a delegate to the Continental Congress and was the main writer of the Declaration of Independence. Jefferson also contributed to the Constitution by suggesting that the Bill of Rights be added. Before he was elected president, Jefferson served in state government as a delegate to Virginia's legislature and governor of Virginia, and served in federal government as Washington's Secretary of State and Adams's vice president. Thomas Jefferson had a wife, Martha, and two children. Jefferson and his family lived at a house that he designed in Virginia called Monticello. At home, Jefferson enjoyed gardening, playing music, writing, and inventing new things. While he was president, Thomas Jefferson made the Louisiana Purchase, which doubled the size of the United States. He sent Lewis and Clark on their famous expedition to explore the new land. Before he died, Jefferson founded the University of Virginia.

Fill in the correct words below. Then, write the first letter of each word from top to bottom to learn one thing that Thomas Jefferson invented.

1. served as Washington's Secretary of ___ ___ ___ ___ ___

2. studied at the College of ___ ___ ___ ___ ___ ___ ___ and Mary

3. wrote the Declaration of

   ___ ___ ___ ___ ___ ___ ___ ___ ___ ___ ___ ___

4. was the governor of ___ ___ ___ ___ ___ ___ ___ ___

5. asked Lewis and Clark to ___ ___ ___ ___ ___ ___ ___ the Louisiana Territory

6. made the ___ ___ ___ ___ ___ ___ ___ ___ ___ Purchase

7. was a delegate to the Continental ___ ___ ___ ___ ___ ___ ___ ___

8. Monticello was his ___ ___ ___ ___ ___.

9. born on ___ ___ ___ ___ ___ 13, 1743

10. was an ___ ___ ___ ___ ___ ___ ___ ___ ___ ___ ___ and well-educated man

11. suggested the Bill of ___ ___ ___ ___ ___ ___

Thomas Jefferson invented the ___ ___ ___ ___ ___ ___ ___ ___ ___ ___ ___.

James Madison

4th President
Born: March 16, 1751 in Port Conway, Virginia
Political Party: Democratic-Republican
Term of Office: two terms from March 4, 1809 to March 3, 1817
Vice Presidents: George Clinton (first term) and Elbridge Gerry (second term)
Died: June 28, 1836

James Madison is often called the Father of the Constitution. As a delegate to the Continental Congress, Madison pushed for a new Constitution to replace the weak Articles of Confederation. He believed strongly in the separation of powers and came up with the Virginia Plan, which described three branches of government and a two-house legislature. With some changes, Madison's plan became the basis for the Constitution. Madison was respected as a very smart man. He studied law at the College of New Jersey, which is now called Princeton. Before he became president, he served in the U.S. House of Representatives and as Jefferson's Secretary of State. Madison's wife, Dolley, was one of the country's most beloved first ladies. During Madison's presidency, the U.S. went to war again with the British in the War of 1812. The British captured Washington, D. C., and set fire to the White House. Dolley Madison was able to save a famous painting of George Washington before the house burned down. In 1814, Madison signed the treaty that ended the war, and the capital was returned to Americans.

James Madison was one of the main writers of a series of essays written to convince the states to ratify the Constitution.

Cross out every other letter from left to right starting with W to find out the name of these essays. Write the name on the lines below.

T	W	H	R	E	P	F	D	E	C	D	Q

E	N	R	K	A	V	L	Z	I	U	S	J

T	F	P	H	A	T	P	L	E	W	R	M	S

_____   _____   _____

James Monroe

5th President
Born: April 28, 1758 in Westmoreland County, Virginia
Political Party: Democratic-Republican
Term of Office: two terms from March 4, 1817 to March 3, 1825
Vice President: Daniel Tompkins
Died: July 4, 1831

James Monroe fought bravely alongside George Washington in the Revolutionary War. He also studied law with Thomas Jefferson at the College of William and Mary. Monroe and Jefferson were close friends and had many of the same ideas about government. They both supported the Bill of Rights. Before he became president, James Monroe served as a senator and as governor of Virginia. He served as a diplomat in France and helped Thomas Jefferson make the Louisiana Purchase. Many important things happened for the U.S. during Monroe's presidency. Monroe bought Florida from Spain and helped settle arguments with the British about the Canadian border. In 1820, Monroe signed the Missouri Compromise, which accepted two new states into the Union. One state, Missouri, was accepted as a slave state as long as the other state, Maine, was a free state. Another important contribution Monroe made as president was to write the Monroe Doctrine. The Monroe Doctrine called for European countries to stop setting up new colonies in the Americas. James Monroe had a wife, Elizabeth, and two daughters and was a popular president.

Find the following words about James Monroe in the word search below: lawyer, senator, governor, soldier, president, diplomat, compromise, Florida, Missouri, Maine, border, Bill of Rights, popular.

```
J A V R E I D L O S D X V W G S G B X O T
F S I R U O S S I M T A U T C I W C N Z N
F G P O P U L A R D Z J D U K P Q I I T G
Q B O M A I N E S R P G A I E J P W H X O
S O X D S F J V B I L L O F R I G H T S V
N R X P V X B R R E Y W A L J O A E J M E
R D I X K Y C O M P R O M I S E L G W L R
V E R E Z E R R O T A N E S F A X F Q X N
A R T A M O L P I D P H L P Z W M T I R O
P X S L V Z R X D G T T N E D I S E R P R
```

John Quincy Adams

6th President
Born: July 11, 1767 in Braintree, Massachusetts
Political Party: Democratic-Republican
Term of Office: one term from March 4, 1825 to March 3, 1829
Vice President: John C. Calhoun
Died: February 23, 1848

The son of John Adams, John Quincy Adams lived and traveled throughout Europe, learning different languages and customs. He graduated from Harvard with a law degree and practiced law before he became a U.S. diplomat in Europe and Russia. Adams married a woman he met in Europe, Louisa Johnson, and they had three sons. Adams served as a senator and then as Monroe's Secretary of State. When he ran for president, he did not win the popular vote, Andrew Jackson did. But, no candidate won the majority of electoral votes, so the House of Representatives chose the president. John Quincy Adams won by one vote. Adams had plans for increased trade, new roads, and new schools, but he had a hard time getting his ideas through Congress. After his term as president, Adams served as a congressman in the House of Representatives for nine straight terms.

Circle true or false for each statement. Then, rewrite each false statement to make it true.

1. John Quincy Adams's father was a U.S. president.   true   false

_____

2. Adams graduated from the College of William and Mary.   true   false

_____

3. Adams was a diplomat in China.   true   false

_____

4. Adams was Monroe's Secretary of State.   true   false

_____

5. John Quincy Adams was elected president in the popular vote.   true   false

_____

6. Adams served as a senator for nine terms.   true   false

_____

7. Congress helped Adams accomplish many of his goals for the country.   true   false

_____

Andrew Jackson

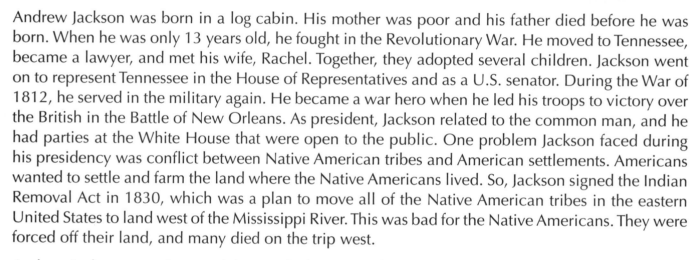

7th President
Born: March 15, 1767 in Waxhaw District, South Carolina
Political Party: Democratic
Term of Office: two terms from March 4, 1829 to March 3, 1837
Vice Presidents: John C. Calhoun (first term) and Martin Van Buren (second term)
Died: June 8, 1845

Andrew Jackson was born in a log cabin. His mother was poor and his father died before he was born. When he was only 13 years old, he fought in the Revolutionary War. He moved to Tennessee, became a lawyer, and met his wife, Rachel. Together, they adopted several children. Jackson went on to represent Tennessee in the House of Representatives and as a U.S. senator. During the War of 1812, he served in the military again. He became a war hero when he led his troops to victory over the British in the Battle of New Orleans. As president, Jackson related to the common man, and he had parties at the White House that were open to the public. One problem Jackson faced during his presidency was conflict between Native American tribes and American settlements. Americans wanted to settle and farm the land where the Native Americans lived. So, Jackson signed the Indian Removal Act in 1830, which was a plan to move all of the Native American tribes in the eastern United States to land west of the Mississippi River. This was bad for the Native Americans. They were forced off their land, and many died on the trip west.

Andrew Jackson was given a nickname for being rough and tough.

Write the missing word in each sentence. Then, write the numbered letters in order below to learn Jackson's nickname.

1. Jackson was born in South ___ ___ ___ ___ ___ ___ ___ ___.
                                  1   2

2. He fought in the Revolutionary War when he was only 13 years ___ ___ ___.
                                                                        3

3. Jackson invited the public to parties at the ___ ___ ___ ___ ___ House.
                                                    4   5

4. ___ ___ ___ ___ ___ ___ ___ signed the Indian Removal Act in 1830.
      6   7

5. Jackson won the Battle of New ___ ___ ___ ___ ___ ___ ___.
                                    8   9

6. Jackson was a ___ ___ ___ ___ ___ ___ ___ ___ hero.
                                               10

___ ___ ___   ___ ___ ___ ___ ___ ___ ___

Martin Van Buren

8th President
Born: December 5, 1782 in Kinderhook, New York
Political Party: Democratic
Term of Office: one term from March 4, 1837 to March 3, 1841
Vice President: Richard Johnson
Died: July 24, 1862

Martin Van Buren was born to a Dutch family in New York state. His father owned an inn in New York, and as a boy, Martin listened to the conversations of the politicians that stayed at the inn. At 14, Van Buren worked in a law office, and by the time he was 21, he was a lawyer. Before he became Andrew Jackson's Secretary of State, Martin Van Buren served in New York government, as a state senator, a U.S. senator, and as governor of New York. As Jackson's vice president, Van Buren worked to form and strengthen the Democratic Party. Martin and his wife, Hannah, had four sons who grew up to become important advisors to their father. During Van Buren's presidency, the U.S. was experiencing hard times. During this depression, many Americans lost their jobs. This made Van Buren unpopular with voters, and he did not win the election to serve a second term.

Decide whether each statement is fact or opinion.

1. The U.S. experienced a depression during Van Buren's presidency.   fact   opinion

2. Martin liked to listen to politicians at his father's inn.   fact   opinion

3. Van Buren was Andrew Jackson's vice president.   fact   opinion

4. Van Buren was very smart.   fact   opinion

5. The Democratic Party was the best political party.   fact   opinion

6. Martin and Hannah Van Buren had four sons.   fact   opinion

7. By the end of his presidency, all Americans disliked Van Buren.   fact   opinion

8. Van Buren was a good president.   fact   opinion

William Henry Harrison

9th President
Born: February 9, 1773 in Charles City County, Virginia
Political Party: Whig
Term of Office: one month from March 4, 1841 to April 4, 1841
Vice President: John Tyler
Died: April 4, 1841

William Henry Harrison had the shortest presidency of any U.S. president. During his inauguration outside in the cold, he got very sick, and died a month after taking office. Harrison had been a military leader. President Adams chose him to be the governor of a large area of Native American territory in present day Indiana and Illinois. He held this position for 12 years, battling the Native Americans and making deals to take away much of their land. Harrison got his nickname, Old Tippecanoe, for fighting Native Americans at Tippecanoe Creek. Because of his success at Tippecanoe, he became a general in the War of 1812. After the war, he served as an Ohio state senator, a U.S. representative for Ohio, and a U.S. senator. Harrison helped to organize the Whig political party. The Whigs did not like Andrew Jackson and his politics, so they formed their own party and put their own candidates up for election to try to beat Jackson's vice president, Van Buren. They did not win the first time, but Harrison finally beat Van Buren in the next election. William Harrison was the first president to run an election campaign similar to the way candidates do today. His campaign used advertising, had slogans, and hosted parties. His famous campaign slogan was "Old Tippecanoe and Tyler too." Harrison had a wife, Anna, and eight children.

Use the Internet and other resources to find out the campaign slogans of other U.S. presidents.

1. Abraham Lincoln: _____

_____

2. Calvin Coolidge: _____

3. Herbert Hoover: _____

_____

4. Dwight Eisenhower: _____

5. George H. W. Bush: _____

John Tyler

10th President
Born: March 29, 1790 in Charles City County, Virginia
Political Party: Whig
Term of Office: almost one full term from April 6, 1841 to March 3, 1845
Vice President: none
Died: January 18, 1862

John Tyler was never elected to be the president of the United States. As William Harrison's vice president, Tyler became president when Harrison died. Tyler studied at the College of William and Mary and worked as a lawyer before he entered politics. He first served in Virginia state government and later in Congress as a representative and a senator. Tyler was part of the anti-Jackson group that formed the Whig Party. After he became president, he decided he did not agree with the Whigs either. Tyler vetoed many bills and made Congress very mad at him. He did make some important decisions while he was president. He started trade with China and added Texas as a new state. Tyler's wife died during his presidency, and he remarried, becoming the first president to marry while in office. Between his two marriages, Tyler had 14 children. After he served out Harrison's term as president, Tyler moved back to Virginia and supported the southern states leaving the Union.

Answer the following questions.

1. How did John Tyler become the president of the United States? _____

_____

2. What U.S. document states the law for how Tyler became president? _____

_____

3. What was one important thing that John Tyler did as president? _____

_____

4. Why didn't Tyler get along with Congress? _____

_____

5. What war resulted from what Tyler wanted the southern states to do? _____

_____

James K. Polk

11th President
Born: November 2, 1795 in Mecklenburg County, North Carolina
Political Party: Democratic
Term of Office: one term from March 4, 1845 to March 3, 1849
Vice President: George M. Dallas
Died: June 15, 1849

James K. Polk was a strong president. He got many important things done for the United States. When James Polk was a boy, his family moved in a covered wagon to Tennessee. He graduated from the University of North Carolina and became interested in politics. Polk served in Tennessee government for a few years before he was elected to the U.S. House of Representatives. He served in the House for six terms and served as Speaker of the House for four years. James Polk was also the governor of Tennessee for one term. His wife, Sarah, was an intelligent and sociable woman who took well to the life of a politician's wife. During the presidential election, Polk was thought of as the *dark horse candidate*, or a candidate who is not well-known but might be able to win. His opponent's campaign slogan was "Who is James K. Polk?" As president, Polk wanted to expand the U.S. from ocean to ocean, and he did. He added California and New Mexico to the U.S. as a result of the Mexican War. He also added Washington and Oregon to the U.S. by settling problems with the British over the Canadian border.

Fill in the missing words to complete the sentences.

1. James Polk served _____ terms as a U.S. representative from _____.

2. While in the House of Representatives, Polk served as _____ _____

   _____ _____ for four years.

3. James Polk was a _____ _____ candidate.

4. Polk added the states _____ , _____ ,

   _____ , and _____ to the U.S. during

   his presidency.

5. James K. Polk belonged to the _____ Party.

Zachary Taylor

12th President
Born: November 24, 1784 in Orange County, Virginia
Political Party: Whig
Term of Office: less than one term from March 4, 1849 to July 9, 1850
Vice President: Millard Fillmore
Died: July 9, 1850

A military hero, Zachary Taylor was the first president to have no political experience before becoming president. Taylor joined the army as a young man and served through several wars. He became a general and was a hero in the Mexican War when he led his troops to victory over General Santa Anna. After the war, the Whig Party asked him to be their presidential candidate. Arguments between the north and the south over slavery were getting worse as Taylor took office. The government needed to decide whether the new states to the U.S. would be free states or would allow slavery. Up until then, there were 15 free states and 15 slave states. Unfortunately, Taylor got sick and did not live long enough to do much about the problem.

Find the words in the Word Bank in the puzzle below.

```
A V X W G W R W R I A Q L Q P G D V F B X
K Y M L V Y G F Y S H E R O N O U I E Q P
I B Q E F H R G N S C V E X J T W C R K H
F P R X H T F E Y A V I D E I D C T T A F
L X W D R U U N V U C B U W R U P O P U W
J L W A W O S E T A D I I C M F N R D D W
Y T G J A S K R N R L D X K C Y F Y C D H
Q Z A R M Y Y A F I G S Q E H F Z W U N I
S J D S F J A L H T R O N Z M R U O G Z G
```

<table>
<tr><td colspan="4" align="center">**Word Bank**</td></tr>
<tr><td>slavery</td><td>north</td><td>south</td><td>hero</td></tr>
<tr><td>Mexican</td><td>war</td><td>Whig</td><td>general</td></tr>
<tr><td>Army</td><td>victory</td><td>free</td><td>died</td></tr>
</table>

Millard Fillmore

13th President
Born: January 7, 1800 in Cayuga County, New York
Political Party: Whig
Term of Office: less than one term from July 10, 1850 to March 3, 1853
Vice President: none
Died: March 8, 1874

Millard Fillmore's family was very poor. He had to go to work as an apprentice for a cloth maker when he was only 14. Fillmore taught himself how to read, and he read everything he could get his hands on. He went to school briefly before becoming a clerk for a judge. There, he studied law and became a lawyer. Then, he served in the New York state government and later in the U.S. House of Representatives. In 1849, Fillmore was elected as vice president for Zachary Taylor. He and Taylor had not even met until after the election. Unfortunately, they did not get along and disagreed about many issues. After Taylor died, Millard Fillmore became the president. The country was unsettled over the issue of slavery and the new states and territories in the west. Fillmore signed the Compromise of 1850, which allowed California to be a free state and the New Mexico and Utah territories to decide for themselves. The Compromise also included the Fugitive Slave Act, which said that a runaway slave found anywhere in the U.S. would be returned to his owner. The north was upset by this "compromise," which seemed to favor southern slave states. The Compromise of 1850 kept the states from going to war for a little while longer but did not solve the problem. Fillmore also worked to open trade with Japan. His wife and former teacher, Abigail, started the White House library.

Fill in the blanks.

1. At 14, Fillmore worked as a cloth maker's _____.

2. Fillmore taught himself to read and became a _____.

3. Millard Fillmore served in the U.S. House of _____.

4. Fillmore was elected as Taylor's _____ president.

5. The country was divided about the issue of _____.

6. Fillmore signed the _____ of 1850.

7. _____ was to be a free state.

8. The _____ Slave Act returned runaway slaves to their owners.

9. Fillmore opened _____ with Japan.

10. Abigail Fillmore started a _____ in the White House.

Franklin Pierce

14th President
Born: November 23, 1804 in Hillsborough, New Hampshire
Political Party: Democratic
Term of Office: one term from March 4, 1853 to March 3, 1857
Vice President: none; William R. King died before term began
Died: October 8, 1869

Use the words in the Word Bank to complete the paragraph.

Franklin Pierce was a lawyer who started his _____ career in

New Hampshire government. He was a _____ in the U.S.

House of Representatives and was a U.S. _____. His

_____ , Jane, did not like the political life and did not want to live in Washington.

So, Pierce left the senate. He joined the _____ during the Mexican War and

worked his way up to _____ . After the war, he went

back to practicing _____ in New Hampshire. Pierce was

_____ by the _____ Party to run for president,

and he easily won the _____. Unfortunately, his _____

president, William King, died before their term began. As president, Pierce wanted to

keep the _____ together, but things only got _____ ,

especially when he _____ the Kansas-Nebraska Act. This act allowed

the _____ in Kansas and Nebraska to decide for themselves whether

to allow _____ in their territories.

Word Bank

law	general	congressman	slavery	political
Democratic	nominated	country	Army	election
signed	vice	worse	senator	wife
people				

James Buchanan

15th President
Born: April 23, 1791 in Cove Gap, Pennsylvania
Political Party: Democratic
Term of Office: one term from March 4, 1857 to March 3, 1861
Vice President: John C. Breckenridge
Died: June 1, 1868

Like many presidents, James Buchanan started out as a lawyer and began his government career in his state's legislature. Buchanan then served Pennsylvania in the U.S. House of Representatives and in the U.S. Senate. He became a diplomat as Minister to Russia and Minister to Great Britain. He was also the secretary of state in James Polk's cabinet. James Buchanan was the only president who never married. Buchanan's niece Harriet Lane acted as first lady during his presidency. Buchanan thought that slavery should be an issue for each state to decide for itself, not the federal government. Many people still thought the federal government should act to stop the spread of slavery, which left room for Lincoln to be elected. After a new president is elected but before he takes office, the old president is often called a *lame duck* president. During Buchanan's lame duck period, seven southern states *seceded* from (left) the Union and formed the Confederacy.

Fill in the missing words below. Then, use the numbered letters to spell out a note that Buchanan gave to Lincoln when he was elected.

1. James Buchanan was born in ___ ___ ___ ___   ___ ___ ___.
   <small>1   2</small>

2. Buchanan started out as a ___ ___ ___ ___ ___ ___.
   <small>3   4</small>

3. He was ___ ___ ___ ___ ___ ___ ___ ___ to Russia and Great Britain.
   <small>5   6   7</small>

4. Buchanan was the only president to never ___ ___ ___ ___ ___.
   <small>8   9</small>

5. He was a U.S. senator for ___ ___ ___ ___ ___ ___ ___ ___ ___ ___ ___ ___.
   <small>10   11   12   13</small>

6. Before he left office, seven ___ ___ ___ ___ ___ ___ ___ states seceded and
   <small>14 15   16</small>

   formed the ___ ___ ___ ___ ___ ___ ___ ___ ___ ___.
   <small>17   18   19</small>

"___ ___ ___ ___ ___ ___ ___ ___ ___ ' ___ ___ ___ ___ ___ ___ ___ ___
<small>5   19   18   1   8   9   6   13   9   13   17   19   14   15   8   9   1</small>

___ ___ ___ ___ ___ ___ ___ ___ ___ ___ ___ ___ ___ ___ ___ ___ ___
<small>8   6   16   8   10 10 19   14 11   1   11   7   1   9   13 11   2</small>

___ ___ ___ ___ ___ ___ ___ ___ ___ ___ ___ ___ ___ ___ ___ ___ ___
<small>7   16   1   4   16 13   7   1   16 14 15   6   1   8   6   13   14 11</small>

___ ___ ___ ___ ___ ___ ___ ' ___ ___ ___ ___ ___ ___ ___ ___
<small>3   1   8   12 13 11   2   19 14 15   8   9   1   8</small>

___ ___ ___ ___ ___ ___ ___ ___ ___ ___ ___ ___ ___ ___ ."
<small>16 8   10 10 19   5   8   11   13 11 18   1   1   18</small>

Abraham Lincoln

16th President
Born: February 12, 1809 in Hardin County, Kentucky
Political Party: Republican
Term of Office: one full term and one partial term from March 4, 1861
                     to April 15, 1865
Vice Presidents: Hannibal Hamlin (first term) and Andrew Johnson (second term)
Died: April 15, 1865

Many people think Abraham Lincoln was the greatest president in American history. He was a strong leader and an honest and moral man. Lincoln was born in a log cabin, and his family did not have much. He learned a lot on his own, studied hard, and became a lawyer and a congressman. Then, Lincoln ran for senator of Illinois. His opponent, Stephen Douglas, won the election, but their debates earned him respect and made it clear that he wanted to stop the spread of slavery. At the beginning of his presidency, 11 southern states had seceded and formed the Confederacy. Confederate troops attacked Fort Sumter, and the Civil War began. The war lasted for four years, but Lincoln kept the Union strong throughout. In 1863, Lincoln issued the Emancipation Proclamation, which freed all slaves in the Confederacy. Also that year, Lincoln gave his famous Gettysburg Address at a Civil War cemetery for Union soldiers. The speech was very inspiring and helped boost the morale of the Union. Finally, in 1865, Confederate General Robert E. Lee surrendered, and the war was over. There was a lot of work still to be done to get the United States back on track, but Abraham Lincoln would not live to do this work. Five days after Lee surrendered, Lincoln was *assassinated*, or killed, while he was watching a play at Ford's Theater.

The following is part of Lincoln's Gettysburg Address. Use a dictionary to rewrite the phrases below.

Fourscore and seven years ago our fathers brought forth on this continent a new nation, conceived in liberty and dedicated to the proposition that all men are created equal . . . . we here highly resolve that these dead shall not have died in vain, that this nation shall have a new birth of freedom, and that government of the people, by the people, for the people shall not perish from the earth.

1. Fourscore and seven years _____

2. brought forth . . . a new nation _____

3. dedicated to the proposition _____

4. shall not have died in vain _____

5. shall not perish _____

Andrew Johnson

17th President
Born: December 29, 1808 in Raleigh, North Carolina
Political Party: National Union
Term of Office: less than one term from April 15, 1865 to March 3, 1869
Vice President: none
Died: July 31, 1875

Andrew Johnson was working as a tailor when he met his wife, Eliza. She taught him how to read and write. He worked his way up in politics from mayor of his town, to member of the Tennessee legislature, to governor of his state, to U.S. congressman. While he was a senator, his home state of Tennessee seceded from the United States along with several other southern states. Johnson believed in states' rights but was against the breakup of the U.S. He stood up against his state and stayed with the Union. President Lincoln chose Johnson to be his vice president for his second term, and when Lincoln was killed, Johnson became president. The Civil War was over, but there were many decisions to make about the rights of former slaves. Johnson still thought the states should have the right to decide for themselves about slavery, and he fought with Congress over bills that gave ex-slaves the same rights as other U.S. citizens. Congress overrode many of Johnson's vetoes and even impeached President Johnson. He was found "not guilty" in the Senate by just one vote. After his term as president was over, Johnson again served as a senator. He has been the only president to do this.

Number the events to put them in the correct order.

1. _____ President Lincoln was assassinated.

2. _____ Johnson worked as a tailor.

3. _____ The Civil War ended.

4. _____ Johnson was elected as vice president.

5. _____ Johnson became the president.

6. _____ Johnson was impeached.

7. _____ The Civil War began.

8. _____ For the second time, Johnson served as a U.S. senator.

9. _____ Johnson was found "not guilty" in the Senate.

Ulysses S. Grant

18th President
Born: April 27, 1822 in Point Pleasant, Ohio
Political Party: Republican
Term of Office: two terms from March 4, 1869 to March 3, 1877
Vice Presidents: Schuyler Colfax (first term) and Henry Wilson (second term)
Died: July 23, 1885

Ulysses Grant graduated from West Point Military Academy and served in the Mexican War. When the war was over, he married Julia Dent and worked at several different jobs before he returned to the army during the Civil War. Grant was a strong and successful military leader, and Lincoln asked him to be in charge of the Union army. Grant's army won many battles, and in April of 1865, the Confederate army's leader, General Robert E. Lee, surrendered to Grant. Ulysses Grant became a hero, which helped him get elected as president. Grant faced many troubles during his presidency. He did not have any experience in government and may not have been the best choice for president. Grant appointed friends to important government positions, and his friends turned out to be irresponsible and dishonest. Grant wanted to run for a third term, but his party did not want to break the tradition of a two-term limit. After his presidency, Grant wrote an autobiography.

Match each word below to the correct definition.

1. graduate

2. academy

3. military

4. surrender

5. experience

6. appoint

7. irresponsible

8. dishonest

9. tradition

10. autobiography

a. school

b. not truthful

c. story about your own life

d. having to do with the armed forces

e. to complete school

f. to give up

g. the way things are done year after year

h. to choose someone for a certain job

i. not dependable

j. knowledge gained through participation and observation

Rutherford B. Hayes

19th President
Born: October 4, 1822 in Delaware, Ohio
Political Party: Republican
Term of Office: one term from March 4, 1877 to March 3, 1881
Vice President: William A. Wheeler
Died: January 1, 1893

Rutherford B. Hayes brought respect and integrity back to the White House. Hayes was an honest and moral man. He was married to an intelligent woman, Lucy Webb, who became the first First Lady to have gone to college. Hayes went to Harvard Law School and became a successful lawyer. When the Civil War began, he left his job and went to fight for the Union. During the war, he ran for the U.S. House of Representatives, but he did not leave the fighting to come home and campaign. This showed great character, and he won the election. After his term in Congress, Hayes served as governor of Ohio. In 1876, Hayes ran for president. The election was very close in some states, and a special group in Congress was assigned to look at the results. They decided that the electoral votes for the contested states should go to Hayes, and he won the election. When Hayes became president, the country was in a period of reconstruction after the Civil War. He worked to pull the country back together and ensure the rights of African-American citizens.

Choose the correct answer for each question.

1. Lucy Hayes was the first First Lady to have done what?
   a. ride in a car   b. fly a plane   c. be a lawyer   d. go to college

2. What war did Hayes fight in?
   a. World War I   b. Revolutionary   c. Civil   d. Mexican

3. Hayes was elected to what office while he was still fighting in the war?
   a. senator   b. president   c. governor   d. representative

4. Who declared Hayes the winner of the presidential election?
   a. Grant   b. Congress   c. Supreme Court   d. the First Lady

5. What did Hayes want to do during his presidency?
   a. ensure the rights of African-Americans   c. neither a nor b
   b. pull the country back together   d. both a and b

6. Which of the following best describes Rutherford Hayes?
   a. honest and moral   b. uneducated   c. irresponsible   d. cowardly

James A. Garfield

20th President
Born: November 19, 1831 in Orange, Ohio
Political Party: Republican
Term of Office: less than one term from March 4, 1881
              to September 17, 1881
Vice President: Chester Arthur
Died: September 17, 1881

Growing up, James Garfield worked on his family's farm. He took odd jobs to work his way through school. After graduating from Williams College, Garfield worked as a teacher and president of a college in Ohio. He was married to Lucretia Rudolph, and they had four children. Garfield was against slavery and the breakup of the Union, so he joined the Union army to fight in the Civil War. During the war, Garfield fought many battles and became a general. He was elected to the U.S. House of Representatives and served nine terms. He was nominated for president by the Republican Party and won the election in a close race. Garfield did not have much time in office—he was shot just four months after his inauguration. Garfield lived for two more months before he died.

Use the information from the paragraph or do additional research to complete the acrostic poem about James A. Garfield. The first two lines have been done fore you.

J oined the Army _____
A gainst slavery _____
M _____
E _____
S _____

A _____

G _____
A _____
R _____
F _____
I _____
E _____
L _____
D _____

Chester A. Arthur

21st President
Born: October 5, 1830 in Fairfield, Vermont
Political Party: Republican
Term of Office: less than one term from September 20, 1881
 to March 3, 1885
Vice President: none
Died: November 18, 1886

Chester Arthur was a preacher's son who was remembered for being very friendly and polite. Arthur taught school to make money while going to college and law school and became an important lawyer in New York. Arthur believed in equal rights for African-Americans and helped defend African-Americans in court. Chester Arthur served as James Garfield's vice president. When Garfield was killed, Arthur became president. People weren't sure whether Arthur would make a good president or not, but he did. Often, presidents appointed friends and people who had done favors for them to government positions. These people weren't always honest or good at their jobs. Arthur worked to pass the Pendleton Civil Service Act, which made people take and pass a test before they could have government jobs. Also during his presidency, Arthur made improvements to the Navy and to the postal service.

Decide whether each statement is fact or opinion by circling the letters under the correct columns. Then, write the circled letters in order below to see Arthur's nickname.

	fact	opinion
1. Chester Arthur was the smartest president.	An	Th
2. Arthur became president when Garfield was killed.	e	Exc
3. Arthur liked going to school.	e	Ge
4. Chester Arthur made a good president.	lle	ntl
5. People who want something for doing a favor are mean.	nt	em
6. Arthur passed a law requiring civil servants to pass a test.	an	Lea
7. Arthur worked as a lawyer in New York.	B	d
8. Everyone liked Chester Arthur.	er	oss

Arthur's nickname:

____ ____ ____   ____ ____ ____ ____ ____ ____ ____ ____ ____   ____ ____ ____ ____

Grover Cleveland

22nd and 24th President
Born: March 18, 1837 in Caldwell, New Jersey
Political Party: Democratic
Term of Office: two terms from March 4, 1885 to March 3, 1889 and
                from March 4, 1893 to March 3, 1897
Vice Presidents: Thomas Hendricks (first term) and Adlai Stevenson (second term)
Died: June 24, 1908

Grover Cleveland was born Steven Grover Cleveland. Cleveland studied to be a lawyer. Then, he worked as the sheriff of Erie County, New York. He did such a good job that he was elected mayor of Buffalo, New York. As mayor, Cleveland fought people who were dishonest in politics and business. Hoping that he would do the same for the state of New York, the people elected him as governor. Cleveland became known as a strong and honest leader, which helped him win the presidency. As president, Cleveland was strict with the budget and often fought with Congress by using his veto power. He vetoed over 500 bills during his two terms as president. At the end of his first term, the country was in a deep depression—many people were out of work—and Cleveland did not win reelection. He did, however, come back to win the next election. He is the only president who served two terms that were not *consecutive*, or one right after the other. Cleveland was also the only president to be married in the White House. His wife, Frances, was a young and popular first lady. Their second daughter, Esther, was the first child born in the White House.

Fill in the answers and missing words below to read the name of a candy bar that was named after Cleveland's first child.

1. Cleveland was mayor of what city? __ __ __ __ __ __ __

2. Cleveland was a strong and honest _____. __ __ __ __ __ __ __

3. He kept the country on a strict _____. __ __ __ __ __ __

4. He was the governor of what state? __ __ __ __ __ __ __

5. The country was in a _____. __ __ __ __ __ __ __ __ __

6. His wife was a _____ first lady. __ __ __ __ __ __ __

7. What executive power did he use a lot? __ __ __ __

8. He was the only president to be married here. __ __ __ __ __ __ __ __ __ __ __

Cleveland's first child: __ __ __ __   __ __ __ __

Benjamin Harrison

23rd President
Born: August 20, 1833 in North Bend, Ohio
Political Party: Republican
Term of Office: one term from March 4, 1889 to March 4, 1893
Vice President: Levi P. Morton
Died: March 13, 1901

Benjamin Harrison was the grandson of the ninth president, William Henry Harrison. As a boy, Harrison loved to read and learn as much as he could. Harrison worked as a lawyer before he fought in the Civil War. After the war, he ran for governor of Ohio but did not win the election. Instead, he became a U.S. senator for Indiana. When he ran for president, he did not win the popular vote, but he won enough electoral votes to be named the new president. During his presidency, Harrison built up the Navy and worked to give more government benefits to Civil War veterans. He also wanted to protect the rights of Native Americans and African-Americans. Harrison signed treaties to increase trade with other countries and worked toward strengthening relationships with other countries in the Americas. Electric lights were put into the White House during Harrison's presidency. His wife, Caroline, put up the first Christmas tree in the White House.

Unscramble the names of the six states that joined the Union when Harrison was president.

1. H N O R T   A A D K O T

_____

2. A G H I N N O S T W

_____

3. A D H I O

_____

4. A A M N N O T

_____

5. H O S T U   A A D K O T

_____

6. G I M N O W Y

_____

William McKinley

25th President
Born: January 29, 1843 in Niles, Ohio
Political Party: Republican
Term of Office: less than two terms from March 4, 1897 to
September 14, 1901
Vice Presidents: Garret A. Hobart (first term) and Theodore Roosevelt
(second term)
Died: September 14, 1901

William McKinley was the last president to have served in the Civil War. After the war, he went back to school to become a lawyer. McKinley wanted to get into politics, so he ran for the U.S. House of Representatives. He served two terms as a congressman for Ohio. While he was a congressman, he supported high taxes on products imported from other countries to help keep jobs for Americans. Before he became president, he was elected to two terms as governor of Ohio. McKinley did not travel much during his campaign because his wife, Ida, was sick, and he didn't want to leave her. When McKinley was president, the United States went to war with Spain to help Cuba get its independence. McKinley helped the U.S. become a world power. In September after the start of his second term as president, William McKinley was assassinated.

Find the words in the Word Bank in the puzzle below.

```
K H L Y R A S S A S S I N A T E D J O C S
W S K M I M L L M O Z N R A W A M E H D F
A H Y D V W N A M S S E R G N O C W I C P
Z C L E J F D W Y G P T F V H T K E O U Y
K F X G Q C Q Y Z P X A W U S A C Y L B Y
R S U R O N R E V O G A I D D X N R D A Z
W W J B H M P R E S I D E N T E X J C S D
S W A W P D J J O B S O R T E S R E W O P
```

Word Bank			
president	lawyer	congressman	taxes
governor	Cuba	Spain	war
power	assassinated	Ohio	jobs

Theodore Roosevelt

26th President
Born: October 27, 1858 in New York, New York
Political Party: Republican
Term of Office: less than two terms from September 14, 1901 to
          March 3, 1909
Vice President: Charles W. Fairbanks
Died: January 6, 1919

Theodore Roosevelt was a strong and adventurous man. After graduating from Harvard, he was elected as a New York state assemblyman. When both his wife and mother died, he decided to get away for a while. He went out west and worked as a cattle rancher and a frontier sheriff. When he returned to New York, he held several important positions in the state government. Adventure called again, and Roosevelt went to fight in the Spanish-American War. He volunteered to fight with a group called the Rough Riders. They won a famous battle at San Juan Hill. After the war, Roosevelt was elected as governor of New York. Then, he served as McKinley's vice president. When McKinley was killed, Roosevelt became president. Theodore Roosevelt did many important things as president. He promoted the building of the Panama canal, set aside millions of acres of land for national forests and wildlife preserves, helped workers, and fought unfair business practices. Roosevelt also was the first president to win a Nobel Peace Prize when he helped make peace between Russia and Japan. He is famous for quoting a proverb to describe how he dealt with foreign countries: "Speak softly and carry a big stick." He was a popular president and even had a stuffed animal named after him—the teddy bear!

Circle the letter beside each correct answer. Write the letters in order to read what Roosevelt's favorite expression was. (At the time, this expression meant terrific, first-rate, or excellent.)

1. Roosevelt worked out west as a   A governor.   B sheriff.

2. Roosevelt fought in the Spanish-American War
   with the   U Rough Riders.   V French.

3. Roosevelt was vice president for   L McKinley.   M Lincoln.

4. Roosevelt won the   K lottery.   L Nobel Peace Prize.

5. Roosevelt set aside land to protect   Y wildlife.   Z cattle.

Roosevelt's favorite expression was _____ !

William H. Taft

27th President
Born: September 15, 1857 in Cincinnati, Ohio
Political Party: Republican
Term of Office: one term from March 4, 1909 to March 3, 1913
Vice President: James Sherman
Died: March 8, 1930

William H. Taft graduated from Yale and became a lawyer and a judge. His dream was to become the Chief Justice of the U.S. Supreme Court. His family and his wife wanted him to go into politics. Taft served as the governor of the Philippines (a country of islands in the Pacific that the U.S. owned). Then, Roosevelt asked him to serve in his Cabinet as Secretary of War. Roosevelt supported Taft for president when his term was over. As president, Taft expanded U.S. trade in the Americas and Asia. He also supported the ratification of the Sixteenth Amendment, which called for an income tax. Taft was more comfortable as a judge than as president, and he did not suggest many new laws or policies. He tried to follow what Roosevelt had done but did some things that Roosevelt did not like. So, Roosevelt ran against Taft in the next election. Neither man won. After his presidency, Taft went back to law and eventually fulfilled his dream when President Harding appointed him to Chief Justice of the U.S. Supreme Court. Taft is the only person to have been both president and Chief Justice of the U.S. Supreme Court.

Answer the following questions.

1. Which amendment was ratified during Taft's presidency? What did it state?

   _____

   _____

2. Do you think Taft made a good president? Why or why not?

   _____

   _____

3. Taft finally fulfilled his dream. What was it? What dream do you have?

   _____

   _____

Woodrow Wilson

28th President
Born: December 28, 1856 in Staunton, Virginia
Political Party: Democratic
Term of Office: two terms from March 4, 1913 to March 3, 1921
Vice President: Thomas R. Marshall
Died: February 3, 1924

Woodrow Wilson was a very educated man. He graduated from Princeton, went to law school, and got a doctorate from Johns Hopkins University. He worked as a college professor and then became the president of Princeton University. Before he was president of the United States, he served for two years as governor of New Jersey. Wilson's *platform*, or plan for what he wanted to do as president, was called "the New Freedom." Wilson was able to complete much of his plan, including passing the Federal Reserve Act, which regulated U.S. banks; passing labor laws to protect workers; and restricting big businesses so that small businesses could compete.

During his presidency, World War I started. Wilson tried to keep the U.S. out of the war until Americans died on a British passenger and cargo ship that was attacked by Germans. After the war, Wilson worked for world peace and tried to set up a league of nations to promote peace. For his efforts, Wilson won the Nobel Peace Prize. Near the end of his presidency, Wilson had a stroke and was not able to complete many of his presidential duties. His wife, Edith, became his spokesperson, making her one of the most powerful first ladies in history.

Complete the crossword puzzle.

Across
2. What state was Wilson born in?
4. Wilson passed laws to protect _____.
6. Wilson's _____ was called "the New Freedom."
8. Wilson restricted big _____.

Down
1. Wilson was a college _____.
3. What state was Wilson governor of?
5. Wilson regulated U.S. _____.
7. What did Wilson want for the world?

Warren G. Harding

29th President
Born: November 2, 1865 in Corsica, Ohio
Political Party: Republican
Term of Office: less than one term from March 4, 1921 to August 2, 1923
Vice President: Calvin Coolidge
Died: August 2, 1923

Use the words in the Word Bank to complete the paragraph.

Warren Harding started out as the _____ of an Ohio newspaper.

He got into _____ as an Ohio state senator and served as _____

governor. In 1914, Harding was _____ to the U.S. Senate. He didn't go to

many _____ and didn't get very involved.

When he became _____ , Harding still was not interested in doing

much with his job and depended on his _____ and Congress to run things.

Harding had _____ many of his friends from _____ to

important positions, and unfortunately, several of them turned out to be _____.

There were many _____ during _____'s presidency

because of these men. Harding and his wife decided to take a tour of the _____

states to get away from all of the _____ in Washington. Harding got

_____ on this trip and _____.

Word Bank

Cabinet	politics	died	western
Ohio	president	elected	appointed
troubles	owner	dishonest	sessions
Harding	sick	scandals	lieutenant

Calvin Coolidge

30th President
Born: July 4, 1872 in Plymouth Notch, Vermont
Political Party: Republican
Term of Office: less than two terms from August 3, 1923 to March 3, 1929
Vice President: Charles Dawes
Died: August 2, 1923

Calvin Coolidge was a quiet and serious man. His nickname was Silent Cal. After graduating from Amherst College, Coolidge became a lawyer. He got involved in local politics on city council, in the mayor's office, and in state government. As governor of Massachusetts, he ended a police strike, which won him the nomination for vice president. He served as vice president under Warren Harding until Harding died and Coolidge became president. Coolidge supported stricter laws for immigration and vetoed a bill that would have given government money to farmers in need. He believed that the government should stay out of other people's business—in the U.S. and in other countries. Calvin Coolidge's wife, Grace, was a friendly and popular first lady.

Answer each question below.

1. What was Calvin Coolidge's nickname?
   a. Major Mayor   b. Cool Coolidge   c. Silent Cal   d. Farmers' Foe

2. What is a strike?

   _____

3. True or False: Coolidge thought the government should support programs to give money to people in need.

   _____

4. Coolidge was the governor of _____.

5. Coolidge thought the U.S. should not get involved with the problems of other countries. Do you agree with his position? Why or why not?

   _____

   _____

   _____

Herbert Hoover

31st President
Born: August 10, 1874 in West Branch, Iowa
Political Party: Republican
Term of Office: one term from March 4, 1929 to March 3, 1933
Vice President: Charles Curtis
Died: October 20, 1964

By the time he was nine years old, both of Herbert Hoover's parents had died. He did not have much, but he was determined to go to college. He studied geology at Stanford where he met his wife, Lou, who was also studying geology. Working as a mining engineer, Hoover owned mines and lived all over the world. He became a millionaire. After World War I, Hoover helped to raise money to send food and supplies to needy people in Europe. Hoover worked in the government as the head of the U.S. Food Administration and the U.S. Department of Commerce but did not want to be paid for either job. Hoover did not take his president's salary either—he donated it to charity. During his presidential campaign, Hoover promised Americans "a chicken in every pot and a car in every garage." Unfortunately, not long after he was elected, the stock market crashed, and the U.S. went into the Great Depression. Many Americans lost their jobs and their homes. Hoover thought the economy would get better if he helped businesses and farmers and gave loans to states to provide food for the unemployed. But, the depression just got worse, and Hoover was not reelected.

Write a T for true or an F for false beside each statement below.

_____ 1. Herbert Hoover inherited his money from his family.

_____ 2. Herbert Hoover studied geology.

_____ 3. Hoover helped raise money to feed people in Europe after the war.

_____ 4. Hoover made a lot of his money from his jobs in the U.S. government.

_____ 5. While Hoover was president, the country went into the Great Depression.

_____ 6. Herbert Hoover was able to keep his campaign promise.

_____ 7. The stock market crashed right before Hoover became president.

_____ 8. Hoover wanted to improve the economy by helping businesses.

_____ 9. Hoover was elected to a second term as president.

Franklin D. Roosevelt

32nd President
Born: January 30, 1882 in Hyde Park, New York
Political Party: Democratic
Term of Office: less than four terms from March 4, 1933 to April 12, 1945
Vice Presidents: John Garner (first two terms), Henry Wallace (third term),
                   Harry Truman (fourth term)
Died: April 12, 1945

Franklin D. Roosevelt (FDR) was elected to four terms as president and served longer than any other U.S. president. Roosevelt graduated from Harvard and went to Columbia Law School. He got into politics as a New York state senator. In 1921, Roosevelt got polio, and he lost the use of his legs. He dropped out of politics for a while but ran for president in 1932 and won. Roosevelt had big plans for getting the country out of the Great Depression. Roosevelt's plan was called the New Deal. The New Deal included starting Social Security, creating public works projects (building roads and parks) to give people jobs, and setting a minimum wage for workers. Roosevelt also talked to Americans on the radio in his "fireside chats" to help keep their spirits up and give them hope. In 1941, the U.S. entered World War II. Roosevelt led the United States through the war and helped the U.S. become a strong world power. Roosevelt died just weeks before the end of the war.

Answer the questions. Use the numbered letters to spell out a quotation from FDR.

1. Roosevelt was elected to how many terms as president?   __ __ __ __
                                                              1

2. Roosevelt lost the use of his legs because of what disease?   __ __ __ __ __
                                                                              2

3. What was the name of FDR's plan?   __ __ __   __ __ __   __ __ __ __
                                              3   4

4. This program gives money to the people over 65.   __ __ __ __ __ __ __
                                                        5   6

    __ __ __ __ __ __ __ __ __
                            7

5. What were FDR's radio talks called?   __ __ __ __ __ __ __ __ __ __ __
                                                  8   9   10 11

6. What university did Roosevelt go to?   __ __ __ __ __ __ __ __
                                                     12

7. This is the least that workers must be paid.   __ __ __ __ __ __ __ __ __ __
                                                            13   14 15

"__ __ __ __ __ __ __ __ __ __ __ __ __ __ __ __ __ __
 11 10 9   2 3 4 7   11 10 13 3 15 14 9   10 6 12 9

__ __ __ __ __ __ __ __ __ __ __ __ __ __ __ __ __ __ __."
11 2   1 9 6 8   13 5   1 9 6 8   13 11 5 9 4 1

Harry S. Truman

33rd President
Born: May 8, 1884 in Lamar, Missouri
Political Party: Democratic
Term of Office: less than two terms from April 12, 1945 to January 20, 1953
Vice President: Alben Barkley
Died: December 26, 1972

Harry Truman grew up working on his family's farm. After fighting in World War I, Truman came back home, married his girlfriend, Bess, and opened a small shop. His business didn't do well, so he got involved in local government and even served as a judge. Then, Truman was elected to the U.S. Senate. He was part of a senate committee that investigated defense department spending and saved the U.S. money. When he was elected vice president to Roosevelt, Harry Truman did not think he would soon be the president. But, when Roosevelt died at the beginning of his fourth term, Truman had to take over the job. Truman tried to continue Roosevelt's New Deal programs, which he called a "Fair Deal," and he worked to protect civil rights. World War II was still going on, and Truman made the decision to drop the atomic bomb on two Japanese cities to end the war. After the war, he issued the Truman Doctrine, which said that the U.S. would help other countries fight communism. Harry Truman also started the Central Intelligence Agency (CIA) and the North Atlantic Treaty Organization (NATO).

Harry Truman had a sign on his desk at the White House that had his motto written on it. Circle the first letter, every other letter, and the last letter in the box to read his motto.

T	U	H	W	E	C	B	I	U	L
C	E	K	A	S	I	T	M	O	P
P	R	S	U	H	V	E	L	R	E

Truman's motto: ___ ___ ___   ___ ___ ___ ___ ___   ___ ___ ___ ___ ___   ___ ___ ___ ___.

If the phrase, "to pass the buck" means to pass the responsibility for something onto someone else, what do you think Truman's motto means?

_____

_____

Dwight D. Eisenhower

34th President
Born: October 14, 1890 in Denison, Texas
Political Party: Republican
Term of Office: two terms from January 20, 1953 to January 20, 1961
Vice President: Richard Nixon
Died: March 28, 1969

Dwight Eisenhower was a military leader. He graduated from West Point and trained forces in World War I. During World War II, Eisenhower was in charge of American and Allied forces in Europe. Eisenhower led the D-Day invasion in 1944, which helped to end the war. When the war was over, Eisenhower worked as the president of Columbia University and later as the commander of NATO forces. As president, Dwight Eisenhower worked for peace. He ended the Korean War and had meetings with world leaders to try to keep the peace. Eisenhower also tried to keep the peace at home. In 1954, the U.S. Supreme Court said that all schools should be desegregated. This meant that students of all races should go to school together. When some people tried to keep African-American students from going to school in Arkansas, Eisenhower sent federal troops there to make sure the students could go to school. Eisenhower also started the National Aeronautics and Space Administration (NASA) and had the interstate highway system built.

Put the following events in order.

1. _____ Eisenhower ended the Korean War.

2. _____ Eisenhower graduated from West Point.

3. _____ The Supreme Court said schools should be desegregated.

4. _____ Eisenhower was the president of Columbia University.

5. _____ Eisenhower trained forces during World War I.

6. _____ Eisenhower sent troops to Arkansas.

7. _____ Eisenhower led the D-Day invasion.

8. _____ Eisenhower was the commander of NATO forces.

9. _____ Eisenhower was elected president for the first time.

John F. Kennedy

35th President
Born: May 29, 1917 in Brookline, Massachusetts
Political Party: Democratic
Term of Office: less than one term from January 20, 1961 to
　　　　　　　　November 22, 1963
Vice President: Lyndon Johnson
Died: November 22, 1963

John F. Kennedy graduated from Harvard and then joined the Navy. He fought in World War II and was wounded. While he was in the hospital recovering, he wrote the book *Profiles in Courage,* which won the Pulitzer Prize. Kennedy got into politics as a congressman in the U.S. House of Representatives. Then, he served as a U.S. senator before he was elected as president. John Kennedy and his wife, Jacqueline, were very popular as president and first lady. They supported civil rights and the arts. Kennedy also encouraged space exploration and started the Peace Corps (pronounced "core"). The Peace Corps is a group of American citizens who volunteer to help people around the world. In his inauguration speech, Kennedy said, "Ask not what your country can do for you—ask what you can do for your country." Kennedy also worked to keep other countries from using nuclear weapons. He stopped Russia from bringing nuclear weapons to Cuba. America became involved in the Vietnam War in 1961 when Kennedy sent troops to assist South Vietnam in a civil war with North Vietnam. John F. Kennedy was assassinated in 1963 while he rode with his wife in a *motorcade*, or parade of cars, in Dallas, Texas.

Circle the best answer to complete each sentence.

1. After Kennedy graduated from college, he joined the _____.
   a. Army　　　　　　　b. Navy　　　　　　　c. Marines　　　　　　d. Peace Corps

2. Kennedy wanted to keep countries from using _____ weapons.
   a. nuclear　　　　　　b. deadly　　　　　　c. American　　　　　d. Russian

3. As a writer, Kennedy won a _____.
   a. gold medal　　　　　b. Nobel Prize　　　　c. Pulitzer Prize　　　d. Newbery Medal

4. Before he was president, Kennedy served as a _____.
   a. judge　　　　　　　b. congressman　　　　c. mayor　　　　　　d. volunteer

5. In 1963 in Dallas, President Kennedy was _____.
   a. giving a speech　　b. married　　　　　　c. in a parade　　　　d. assassinated

6. Kennedy kept nuclear weapons out of _____.
   a. Russia　　　　　　　b. America　　　　　　c. Cuba　　　　　　　d. Canada

Lyndon B. Johnson

36th President
Born: August 27, 1908 in Stonewall, Texas
Political Party: Democratic
Term of Office: less than two terms from November 22, 1963 to
                  January 20, 1969
Vice President: Hubert Humphrey
Died: January 22, 1973

After Kennedy was assassinated, Lyndon Johnson was sworn in as president aboard the president's plane, Air Force One. Lyndon Johnson started out in politics in the U.S. House of Representatives. Then, he left Washington to fight in World War II. When he came back to the United States, Johnson was elected to the U.S. Senate for two terms. He served as John Kennedy's vice president until he became president after Kennedy was killed. Johnson wanted to keep up Kennedy's work and expand it. He wanted to make America a "Great Society" by helping the poor and supporting civil rights. Johnson passed several civil rights bills to protect people against discrimination and started Medicare (medical insurance for the elderly) and Head Start (a preschool program). Johnson also appointed the first African-American Supreme Court justice—Thurgood Marshall. Unfortunately, the Vietnam War was going badly during his presidency, and Johnson did not run for reelection.

Write a short definition or description of each item below.

1. Air Force One: _____

2. civil rights: _____

   _____

3. discrimination: _____

   _____

4. justice (as it is used in the paragraph above): _____

   _____

5. insurance: _____

6. society: _____

Richard M. Nixon

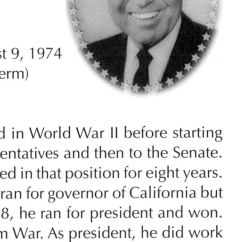

37th President
Born: January 9, 1913 in Yorba Linda, California
Political Party: Republican
Term of Office: less than two terms from January 20, 1969 to August 9, 1974
Vice Presidents: Spiro Agnew (first term) and Gerald Ford (second term)
Died: April 22, 1994

Richard Nixon graduated from Duke Law School and then served in World War II before starting his career in politics. He was elected to the U.S. House of Representatives and then to the Senate. Dwight Eisenhower asked him to be his vice president, and he served in that position for eight years. After that, Nixon ran for president but lost to John Kennedy. Nixon ran for governor of California but lost that election also. Richard Nixon did not give up, and in 1968, he ran for president and won. During his election campaign, Nixon promised to end the Vietnam War. As president, he did work to end the war and signed a peace treaty with North Vietnam (which North Vietnam later broke). Nixon also had important talks with Russia and China. He also withdrew American troops from Vietnam. Nixon did not finish his second term as president. Nixon lied about illegal activities his staff performed for his election campaign, and rather than be impeached and removed from the presidency, he decided to *resign*, or leave the job, on his own.

Circle true or false for each statement. Then, rewrite each false statement to make it true.

1. Richard Nixon was a senator.   true   false

_____

2. Richard Nixon was impeached.   true   false

_____

3. Nixon signed a peace treaty with China.   true   false

_____

4. Nixon was Kennedy's vice president.   true   false

_____

5. Nixon was elected to two terms as president.   true   false

_____

Gerald R. Ford

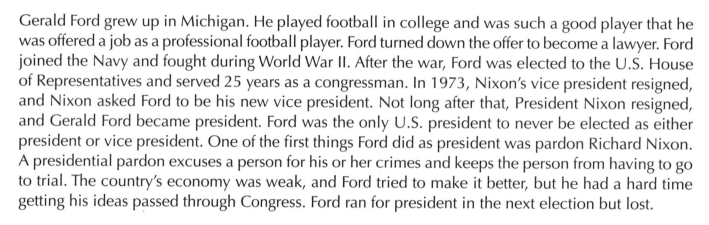

38th President
Born: July 14, 1913 in Omaha, Nebraska
Political Party: Republican
Term of Office: less than one term from August 9, 1974 to January 20, 1977
Vice President: Nelson Rockefeller
Died: December 26, 2006

Gerald Ford grew up in Michigan. He played football in college and was such a good player that he was offered a job as a professional football player. Ford turned down the offer to become a lawyer. Ford joined the Navy and fought during World War II. After the war, Ford was elected to the U.S. House of Representatives and served 25 years as a congressman. In 1973, Nixon's vice president resigned, and Nixon asked Ford to be his new vice president. Not long after that, President Nixon resigned, and Gerald Ford became president. Ford was the only U.S. president to never be elected as either president or vice president. One of the first things Ford did as president was pardon Richard Nixon. A presidential pardon excuses a person for his or her crimes and keeps the person from having to go to trial. The country's economy was weak, and Ford tried to make it better, but he had a hard time getting his ideas passed through Congress. Ford ran for president in the next election but lost.

Write the correct words to complete the sentences.

1. Gerald Ford could have been a professional _____ player.

2. Ford fought in the _____ during World War II.

3. Ford served for 25 years in the _____.

4. Nixon asked Ford to be his _____.

5. Nixon _____ , and Gerald Ford became president.

6. Ford gave Nixon a presidential _____.

7. Ford tried to make the country's _____ better.

8. Ford had trouble getting bills passed in _____.

9. Gerald Ford was never _____ as president or vice president.

James E. Carter, Jr.

39th President
Born: October 1, 1924 in Plains, Georgia
Political Party: Democratic
Term of Office: one term from January 20, 1977 to January 20, 1981
Vice President: Walter Mondale
Died: _____

James Carter, or Jimmy Carter as he is more commonly known, was raised on his family's farm. Carter went to college at the U.S. Naval Academy and served on a submarine in the Navy. After that, he ran for state government and was elected as a state senator. Carter tried to fight against segregation laws in the south. In 1971, he became the governor of Georgia. As president of the United States, Jimmy Carter started the Department of Energy, helped make peace between Israel and Egypt, and fought for human rights around the world. Carter also faced many problems—the economy was declining, there was an energy shortage, and Americans were taken hostage in Iran. Since his presidency, Carter has acted as a diplomat in many countries. Jimmy Carter and his wife, Rosalynn, have also set up groups and programs, such as Habitat for Humanity, to help people in need in the U.S. and around the world.

Write the missing words in the blanks. Then, unscramble the circled letters to find out what important award Carter won in 2002.

1. As president, Carter fought for __ __ __ __(__) rights.

2. Carter faced an __ __(__)__ __ __ shortage.

3. Jimmy and Rosalynn Carter __ __(__)__ people in need around the world.

4. President Carter helped make (__)__ __ __ __ between Israel and Egypt.

5. Before he was governor, Carter served as a state __ __ __ __ __(__)__.

6. Carter was the governor of __ __ __(__)__(__)__.

7. Americans were taken __ __ __ __ __ __(__) in Iran.

Carter won the __ __ b __ __ __ __ __ z __ .

Ronald W. Reagan

40th President
Born: February 6, 1911 in Tampico, Illinois
Political Party: Republican
Term of Office: two terms from January 20, 1981 to January 20, 1989
Vice President: George H. W. Bush
Died: June 5, 2004

Ronald Reagan was the oldest president of the United States and also was the only president to have been a professional actor. Reagan worked for a while as a sportscaster and then became a movie actor. He appeared in over 50 movies and hosted a popular television show. Reagan decided to get into politics, and he ran for governor of California. He won the election and served for eight years. Reagan believed in limiting government and giving people and businesses more freedom. As president of the United States, Ronald Reagan cut taxes, reduced unemployment, and strengthened the military. Reagan also talked many times with Mikhail Gorbachev, the leader of the Soviet Union, and signed an agreement with him to reduce each country's supply of nuclear weapons. Reagan's wife, Nancy, ran a campaign to try to keep kids from taking drugs. Reagan appointed the first woman to the U.S. Supreme Court—Sandra Day O'Connor.

Circle the letter under "fact" or "opinion" for each statement. Then, write the letters in order to see what kind of candy Ronald Reagan liked.

	fact	opinion
1. Ronald Reagan was a good actor.	L	J
2. Reagan was the governor of California.	E	I
3. Limiting government is a smart thing to do.	C	L
4. Everyone in America liked Reagan.	O	L
5. Reagan hosted a television show.	Y	R
6. Sandra Day O'Connor is a good Supreme Court Justice.	I	B
7. Ronald Reagan cut taxes.	E	C
8. Ronald Reagan was a Republican.	A	E
9. Reagan was a better president than an actor.	S	N
10. Reagan had several talks with the Soviet leader.	S	T

Reagan liked ____ ____ ____ ____ ____   ____ ____ ____ ____ ____ .

George H. W. Bush

41st President
Born: June 12, 1924 in Milton, Massachusetts
Political Party: Republican
Term of Office: one term from January 20, 1989 to January 20, 1993
Vice President: Dan Quayle
Died: _____

As a young man, George H. W. Bush studied economics at Yale University and served as a pilot in the Navy during World War II. After the war, he and his wife, Barbara, moved to Texas. Bush became a successful businessman in the oil industry. Then, Bush decided he wanted to get into politics. He was elected to the U.S. House of Representatives. Before he was Reagan's vice president, Bush held many important positions, including Ambassador to the United Nations, U.S. representative to China, and Director of the CIA. President Bush was successful with foreign policy but had a hard time improving the economy in the U.S. Bush helped to end the Cold War (the war against communism). During his presidency, the Soviet Union broke up, and the Berlin Wall was torn down in Germany. Bush took military action in Panama against the corrupt leader Manuel Noriega and led forces to victory over Iraq in the Persian Gulf War.

Answer the following questions.

1. What did George H. W. Bush do during World War II? _____

   _____

2. What did Bush do for a living in Texas before he became a congressman? _____

   _____

3. Bush served as vice president for which president? _____

4. What was the Cold War? _____

   _____

5. What two things happened at the end of the Cold War? _____

   _____

6. Which war did Bush help to win in Iraq? _____

William J. Clinton

42nd President
Born: August 19, 1946 in Hope, Arkansas
Political Party: Democratic
Term of Office: two terms from January 20, 1993 to January 20, 2001
Vice President: Al Gore
Died: _____

William, or Bill, Clinton graduated from Georgetown University and Yale Law School. He also earned a scholarship to study in England for two years. Clinton taught law school for a while, was elected attorney general of Arkansas, and then was elected governor of Arkansas. He served five terms as governor and worked to improve education in his state. When he was elected president, Bill Clinton promised a program that would make sure every American had health insurance. Clinton put his wife, Hillary, in charge of the program, but unfortunately it failed. Clinton was able to reduce the national debt and encourage free trade between the U.S., Canada, and Mexico. Clinton helped keep democracy in Haiti by preventing a dictator from taking over. He also sent the military to help end the conflict and keep the peace in Bosnia. In 1998, Clinton was impeached by the House of Representatives for lying in court, but the Senate found him not guilty.

Answer the following questions.

1. What is a scholarship? What could you say about Bill Clinton for having earned a scholarship?

   _____

   _____

   _____

2. Clinton used the U.S. military to help people in other countries that were in trouble. Do you think the United States should always help other countries? Why or why not?

   _____

   _____

   _____

   _____

George W. Bush

43rd President
Born: July 6, 1946 in Midland, Texas
Political Party: Republican
Term of Office: two terms from January 20, 2001 to January 20, 2009
Vice President: Dick Cheney
Died: _____

The son of George H. W. Bush, George W. Bush studied history at Yale University. He served as a fighter pilot in the Texas Air National Guard. Bush then went back to school to get a business degree from Harvard. He went to work in the oil industry, like his father. Then, along with a group of investors, Bush bought the Texas Rangers baseball team before being elected as governor of Texas. Bush served six years as governor and worked to improve education in his state. In 2000, George W. Bush was elected president of the United States in a very close election. As president, Bush cut taxes and passed a plan to raise the standards in public schools. On September 11, 2001, terrorists attacked the World Trade Center in New York City and the Pentagon in Washington, D. C. President Bush helped America get through the tragedy and declared war on terrorism. He created the Office of Homeland Security to protect the U.S. from future terrorism. In 2003, Bush led the U.S. to war with Iraq to remove the dictator, Saddam Hussein, from power. Bush was reelected in November of 2004.

Answer the following questions.

1. What did George W. Bush study at Harvard?
   a. history   b. science   c. teaching   d. business

2. Bush served six years as _____ of Texas.

3. What is terrorism? _____

   _____

4. True or False: George W. Bush increased taxes. _____

5. What new office did Bush create? _____

6. True or False: Bush owned a baseball team. _____

7. The Pentagon is a government building in _____.
   a. Texas   b. New York City   c. Washington, D. C.

Barack H. Obama

44th President
Born: August 4, 1961 in Honolulu, Hawaii
Political Party: Democratic
Term of Office: two terms from January 20, 2009 to January 20, 2017.
Vice President: Joe Biden
Died: _____

Barack Obama graduated from Columbia University and Harvard Law School. At Harvard, he was the first African American president of the law school's journal. After graduating from law school, Obama moved to Chicago and became a civil rights lawyer. He was also a lecturer at the University of Chicago. He served on the Illinois Senate before being elected to the U.S. Senate in 2004. While he served on the Illinois Senate, Obama helped cut taxes and worked to improve early education in Illinois. During his time in the U.S. Senate, Obama worked to ensure that veterans and soldiers returning from Iraq and Afghanistan were given the benefits they deserved. He also supported working closely with other nations to prevent the use of nuclear weapons. While running for president in 2008, Obama pledged to work for a national healthcare plan for the uninsured and to remove troops from Iraq over a period of 16 months. An important part of Obama's healthcare plan was mandatory healthcare for children. Barack Obama is also dedicated to helping the environment, planning a cap-and-trade system to reduce carbon emissions by 80 percent by 2050. Obama was the first African American major party presidential nominee and the first African American to be elected president. Obama was reelected in November of 2012.

Answer the following questions.

1. What was unique about Barack Obama becoming the president of Harvard Law School's

   journal and the United States? _____

   _____

2. What was an important part of Obama's proposed healthcare plan? _____

   _____

3. What was Barack Obama's plan for the troops in Iraq? _____

   _____

Presidents Quiz

Circle the correct answer for each question.

1. Which president made the Louisiana Purchase?

    a. Madison   b. J. Q. Adams   c. Lincoln   d. Jefferson

2. Which president moved Native Americans from their homes in the east to Oklahoma?

    a. Jackson   b. Monroe   c. Grant   d. Hoover

3. Which president started the Peace Corps?

    a. Reagan   b. Kennedy   c. Carter   d. Nixon

4. Which president was known for using the veto a lot?

    a. Cleveland   b. Polk   c. Garfield   d. F. D. Roosevelt

5. Who was the first president of the United States?

    a. J. Adams   b. Jefferson   c. Washington   d. Madison

6. This former actor made an agreement with the leader of the Soviet Union to reduce the number of weapons each country had.

    a. Reagan   b. Ford   c. Clinton   d. Eisenhower

7. This president became a Supreme Court justice after his presidency.

    a. Arthur   b. Harding   c. Taft   d. Hayes

8. Which president declared a war on terrorism?

    a. Carter   b. Nixon   c. G. W. Bush   d. G. H. W. Bush

9. Which president sent federal troops to Arkansas to make sure African-American students could go to school?

    a. Wilson   b. Madison   c. Grant   d. Eisenhower

10. This president freed the slaves during the Civil War.

    a. Buchanan   b. Lincoln   c. Jackson   d. Cleveland

Presidents Quiz (Cont.)

11. This president is sometimes called the Father of the Constitution.

    a. Madison   b. Jefferson   c. Monroe   d. Washington

12. Which president oversaw the building of the Panama Canal?

    a. F. D. Roosevelt   b. T. Roosevelt   c. Polk   d. McKinley

13. Which president donated his presidential salary to charity?

    a. G. W. Bush   b. Coolidge   c. Hoover   d. Carter

14. This president started Social Security and minimum wage.

    a. Harding   b. L. Johnson   c. Kennedy   d. F. D. Roosevelt

15. Which president established a test for people in government?

    a. Arthur   b. Taft   c. Taylor   d. Fillmore

16. Which president dropped the atomic bomb on Japan in World War II?

    a. Coolidge   b. F. D. Roosevelt   c. Truman   d. Kennedy

17. This president expanded the U.S. to the west coast with the addition of California, New Mexico, Washington, and Oregon.

    a. Pierce   b. Polk   c. Monroe   d. Tyler

18. This president was the only president to resign.

    a. Clinton   b. Ford   c. Reagan   d. Nixon

19. Which president was the general in charge of the Union army during the Civil War?

    a. Grant   b. Harrison   c. Van Buren   d. Jackson

20. Which president led the U.S. to victory in the Persian Gulf War?

    a. G. W. Bush   b. Clinton   c. G. H. W. Bush   d. Reagan

Answer Key

Page 5 school, bank, police car, traffic signs, mail carrier, cell phone, street

Page 6 Answers will vary.

Page 7
1. authority
2. authority
3. no authority
4. no authority
5. authority
6. authority
7. no authority
8. authority
9. no authority
10. authority

Page 9
Matches may include (but are not limited to) the following:
1. f. and l.
2. c. and i.
3. b., g., and h.
4. b. and g.
5. c.
6. e., j., and n.
7. d., e., and m.
8. j. and k.
9. a.

Page 11
1. totalitarian
2. democratic
3. parliamentary
4. royalty
5. direct and indirect
6. oligarchy
7. dictatorship
8. prime minister
9. direct

Page 12 Answers will vary.

Page 13 1. d. 2. a. 3. g. 4. f. 5. b. 6. e. 7. c.

Page 15 Answers will vary.

Page 17
All 50 states should be listed. The first 13 should be Connecticut, Delaware, Georgia, Maryland, Massachusetts, New Hampshire, New Jersey, New York, North Carolina, Pennsylvania, Rhode Island, South Carolina, and Virginia.

Page 18 Answers will vary.

Page 19 1. b. 2. c 3. a. 4. b.

Page 20 Answers will vary.

Page 21 1. e. 2. c. 3. a. 4. f. 5. d. 6. b.

Page 22
1. place where metal is cast
2. false
3. Answers will vary.
4. Answers will vary.

Page 23
1. opinion
2. fact
3. opinion
4. fact
5. opinion
6. fact
7. fact
8. opinion

Page 25
1. 8
2. 1
3. 6
4. 5
5. 9
6. 3
7. 4
8. 7
9. 2

Page 26 Answers will vary.

Page 29
work, Revolutionary, Congress, committee, plan, draft, thirteen, approved, national, independent, one, states, amendment, government, power

Page 33
1. carry out, put into effect, perform
2. make laws
3. form an opinion about or come to a conclusion, decide on a question

Page 34
1. executive
2. impeach and remove the president; approve spending, appointments, and treaties; or override the president's veto
3. judicial
4. veto power, ask for new laws
5. the Senate

Page 35
1. g.
2. d.
3. c.
4. f.
5. e.
6. b.
7. a.

Page 36
Delaware, December 7, 1787; Pennsylvania, December 12, 1787; New Jersey, December 18, 1787; Georgia, January 2, 1788; Connecticut, January 9, 1788; Massachusetts, February 6, 1788; Maryland, April 28, 1788; South Carolina, May 23, 1788; New Hampshire, June 21, 1788; Virginia, June 25, 1788; New York, July 26, 1788; North Carolina, November 21, 1789; Rhode Island, May 29, 1790. These states should be colored: DE, PA, NJ, GA, CT, MA, MD, SC, NH.

Page 37 1. b. 2. d. 3. a.

Pages 38–39
Amendment I: T, F, F, T, T
Amendment II: T
Amendment III: T
Amendment IV: F
Amendment V: T, T, F, T, F
Amendments VI and VII: F, F, T, T, T
Amendment VIII: T, T
Amendment IX: F
Amendment X: T

Page 40
1. Thirteenth
2. vote
3. male
4. citizens
5. protested
6. Civil

Page 41
1. the right to vote
2. 1920
3. right to vote cannot be based on gender
4. Equal Rights Amendment
5. Answers will vary.

Page 42
1. Chief of Staff
2. Press Secretary
3. speech writers
4. visitors office
5. travel office
6. scheduling office
7. office of correspondence
8. photo office
9. White House counsel
10. the President's physician

Page 43 1. b. 2. d. 3. false 4. a. 5. c. 6. d. 7. true

Page 45
1. chief executive
2. chief of state
3. political party leader
4. commander in chief
5. legislative leader
6. chief diplomat

Page 46

Across	Down
4. oval	1. Jefferson
5. bowling	2. rooms
6. burned	3. Washington
8. Pennsylvania	7. Dolley
10. West	9. Adams

Page 47 1. d. 2. e. 3. b. 4. g. 5. f. 6. a. 7. c.

Page 48

1. c.	4. a.	7. b.
2. e.	5. h.	8. g. or i.
3. g. or i.	6. f.	9. d.

Page 49

1. Agriculture
2. State
3. Justice
4. Commerce
5. Labor
6. Transportation
7. Defense
8. Energy
9. Housing & Urban Development
10. Education
11. Interior
12. Veterans Affairs
13. Treasury
14. Health & Human Services
15. Homeland Security

Head of Justice Department: Attorney General

Page 50

1. fact	5. opinion	9. fact
2. opinion	6. fact	10. opinion
3. opinion	7. opinion	
4. fact	8. fact	

Page 51

1. because it gave states with larger populations more votes
2. Answers will vary.
3. an agreement in which each side gets part and gives up part of what they want
4. Answers will vary.
5. Answers will vary.

Page 52

1. Congress	4. six	7. committees
2. laws	5. tie	8. majority
3. senator	6. two	9. approve

Page 53

AL: 7; AK: 1; AZ: 8; AR: 4; CA: 53; CO: 7; CT: 5; DE: 1; FL: 25; GA: 13; HI: 2; ID: 2; IL: 19; IN: 9; IA: 5; KS: 4; KY: 6; LA: 7; ME: 2; MD: 8; MA: 10; MI: 15; MN: 8; MS: 4; MO: 9; MT: 1; NE: 3; NV: 3; NH: 2; NJ: 13; NM 3; NY: 29; NC: 13; ND: 1; OH: 18; OK: 5; OR: 5; PA: 19; RI: 2; SC: 6; SD: 1; TN: 9; TX: 32; UT: 3; VT: 1; VA: 11; WA: 9; WV: 3; WI: 8; WY: 1

Page 54 Washington, laws, Capitol, dome, statue, north, House, inaugurated

Page 55

1. first draft of a law
2. it goes to a committee
3. put it aside
4. false
5. false
6. checks and balances

Page 58

1. defendant	4. witness	7. verdict
2. jury	5. evidence	8. trial
3. civil	6. appeal	9. judge

Page 59

1. no	3. yes	5. no	7. no
2. no	4. yes	6. no	8. yes

Page 60

Federal: declare war, make treaties with other countries, print money, establish armed forces, establish post offices; Both: enforce laws, build roads, take land to make parks, collect taxes, establish courts, borrow money; State: run elections, give licenses for jobs, ratify Constitutional amendments, give marriage licenses, establish public schools

Page 61

1. false	4. true	7. false	10. false
2. true	5. false	8. true	
3. false	6. true	9. true	

Page 62 Students should answer questions for their state.

Page 64 1. d. 2. d. 3. a. 4. d. 5. b. 6. c. 7. c.

Page 66

1. postal service
2. schools
3. medicare
4. libraries
5. roads
6. welfare
7. courts
8. police
9. armed forces
10. public housing
11. prisons
12. scientific research
13. national debt
14. unemployment
15. Social Security

Page 69

AL: 9; AK: 3; AZ: 10; AR: 6; CA: 55; CO: 9; CT: 7; DE: 3; D.C.: 3; FL: 27; GA: 15; HI: 4; ID: 4; IL: 21; IN: 11; IA: 7; KS: 6; KY: 8; LA: 9; ME: 4; MD: 10; MA: 12; MI: 17; MN: 10; MS: 6; MO: 11; MT: 3; NE: 5; NV: 5; NH: 4; NJ: 15; NM: 5; NY: 31; NC: 15; ND: 3; OH: 20; OK: 7; OR: 7; PA: 21; RI: 4; SC: 8; SD: 3; TN: 11; TX: 34; UT: 5; VT: 3; VA: 13; WA: 11; WV: 5; WI: 10; WY: 3

Votes required to win a presidential election: 270

Important states to win: Ohio, Florida, California, Texas, New York

Page 70

1. ideas	4. Democratic	7. state/local
2. two	5. raise	8. needy
3. Republican	6. lower	

Page 71 Answers will vary.

Page 72

1. c.	3. f.	5. d.
2. e.	4. a.	6. b.

Page 73

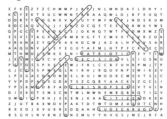

Page 74 Answers will vary.

Page 75

1. 50 states
2. U.S. won independence
3. U.S. Constitution
4. legislative

Page 75 (continued)

5. Thomas Jefferson
6. Supreme Court
7. Answers will vary.
8. Bill of Rights/First Amendment
9. Mayflower
10. amendment
11. Democratic and Republican
12. White House
13. Great Britain

Page 77   Answers will vary.

Page 79

1. George Washington
2. John Adams
3. Thomas Jefferson
4. James Madison
5. James Moore
6. John Quincy Adams
7. Andrew Jackson
8. Martin Van Buren
9. William Henry Harrison
10. John Tyler
11. James K. Polk
12. Zachary Taylor
13. Millard Fillmore
14. Franklin Pierce
15. James Buchanan
16. Abraham Lincoln
17. Andrew Johnson
18. Ulysses S. Grant
19. Rutherford B. Hayes
20. James A. Garfield
21. Chester A. Arthur
22. Grover Cleveland
23. Benjamin Harrison
24. Grover Cleveland
25. William McKinley
26. Theodore Roosevelt
27. William H. Taft
28. Woodrow Wilson
29. Warren G. Harding
30. Calvin Coolidge
31. Herbert Hoover
32. Franklin D. Roosevelt
33. Harry S. Truman
34. Dwight D. Eisenhower
35. John F. Kennedy
36. Lyndon B. Johnson
37. Richard M. Nixon
38. Gerald R. Ford
39. James E. Carter, Jr.
40. Ronald W. Reagan
41. George H. W. Bush
42. William J. Clinton
43. George W. Bush

Page 80

1. Before I became president, I worked as a surveyor, military leader, farmer, etc.
2. I was the first president of the United States.
3. The name of my home was Mount Vernon.
4. I was the commander in chief of the Army during the Revolutionary War.

Page 81

Across
4. Abigail
6. rights
7. Independence
8. Federalist

Down
1. treaty
2. Quincy
3. diplomat
5. France

Page 82

1. State
2. William
3. Independence
4. Virginia
5. explore
6. Louisiana
7. Congress
8. house
9. April
10. intelligent
11. Rights

Jefferson's invention: swivel chair

Page 83   The Federalist Papers

Page 84

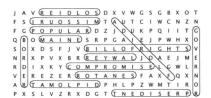

Page 85

1. true
2. false: Adams graduated from Harvard.
3. false: Adams was a diplomat in Europe and Russia.
4. true
5. false: Andrew Jackson won the popular vote.
6. false: Adams served as a congressman for nine terms.
7. false: Adams had a hard time getting his ideas through Congress.

Page 86

1. Carolina
2. old
3. White
4. Jackson
5. Orleans
6. military

Jackson's nickname: Old Hickory

Page 87

1. fact
2. opinion
3. fact
4. opinion
5. opinion
6. fact
7. opinion
8. opinion

Page 88

1. Lincoln: Don't swap horses in the middle of the stream. (or Vote yourself a farm.)
2. Coolidge: Keep cool with Coolidge.
3. Hoover: a chicken in every pot and a car in every garage
4. Eisenhower: I like Ike. (or peace and prosperity)
5. G. H. W. Bush: a kinder, gentler nation

Page 89

1. President Harrison died
2. U.S. Constitution
3. trade with China/added TX to U.S.
4. he vetoed a lot of bills
5. the Civil War

Page 90

1. six, Tennessee
2. Speaker of the House
3. dark horse
4. California, New Mexico, Washington, Oregon
5. Democratic

Page 91

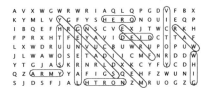

Page 92

1. apprentice
2. lawyer
3. Representatives
4. vice
5. slavery
6. Compromise
7. California
8. Fugitive
9. trade
10. library

Page 93

political, congressman, senator, wife, Army, general, law, nominated, Democratic, election, vice, country, worse, signed, people, slavery

Page 94

1. Cove Gap
2. lawyer
3. minister
4. marry
5. Pennsylvania
6. southern, Confederacy

"My dear sir, if you are as happy on entering the White House as I on leaving, you are a happy man indeed."

Page 95   Answers will vary.

Page 96   1. 4   2. 1   3. 6   4. 3   5. 5   6. 7   7. 2   8. 9   9. 8

Page 97   1. e.   2. a.   3. d.   4. f.   5. j.   6. h.   7. i.   8. b.   9. g.   10. c.

Page 98   1. d.   2. c.   3. d.   4. b.   5. d.   6. a.

Page 99   Answers will vary.

Page 100
1. opinion   4. opinion   7. fact
2. fact   5. opinion   8. opinion
3. opinion   6. fact
Chester Arthur's nickname: The Gentleman Boss

Page 101
1. Buffalo   4. New York   7. veto
2. leader   5. depression   8. White House
3. budget   6. popular
Cleveland's first child: Baby Ruth

Page 102
1. North Dakota   3. Idaho   5. South Dakota
2. Washington   4. Montana   6. Wyoming

Page 103

Page 104
1. sheriff   3. McKinley   5. wildlife
2. Rough Riders   4. Nobel Peace Prize
Roosevelt's favorite expression was Bully!

Page 105
1. Sixteenth—Congress has power to collect income tax
2. Answers will vary.
3. to be a U.S. Supreme Court Justice; answers will vary

Page 106
Across   Down
2. Virginia   1. professor
4. workers   3. New Jersey
6. platform   5. banks
8. business   7. peace

Page 107
owner, politics, lieutenant, elected, sessions, president, Cabinet, appointed, Ohio, dishonest, scandals, Harding, western, troubles, sick, died

Page 108
1. c.
2. Workers refuse to work until employer meets certain demands.
3. false
4. Massachusetts
5. Answers will vary.

Page 109   1. F   2. T   3. T   4. F   5. T   6. F   7. F
              8. T   9. F

Page 110
1. four   3. The New Deal   5. fireside chats
2. polio   4. Social Security 6. Harvard

Page 110 (continued)
7. minimum wage
"The only thing we have to fear is fear itself."

Page 111   Truman's motto: The buck stops here. Answers may vary.

Page 112   1. 7   2. 1   3. 8   4. 4   5. 2   6. 9   7. 3   8. 5   9. 6

Page 113   1. b.   2. a.   3. c.   4. b.   5. d.   6. c.

Page 114
1. the president's plane
2. equality for all, including African-Americans and women
3. denying rights based on race, sex, or religion
4. judge in the Supreme Court
5. a way of paying for health care
6. the people and social systems of a country as a whole

Page 115
1. true
2. false: Nixon resigned.
3. false: Nixon signed a peace treaty with North Vietnam.
4. false: Nixon was Eisenhower's vice president.
5. true

Page 116
1. football   4. vice president   7. economy
2. Navy   5. resigned   8. Congress
3. House of Representatives   6. pardon   9. elected

Page 117
1. human   3. help   5. senator   7. hostage
2. energy   4. peace   6. Georgia
Carter won the Nobel Prize.

Page 118
1. opinion   4. opinion   7. fact   10. fact
2. fact   5. fact   8. fact
3. opinion   6. opinion   9. opinion
Reagan liked jelly beans.

Page 119
1. served as a pilot in the Navy
2. was a businessman in the oil industry
3. Reagan
4. the war against communism
5. Berlin Wall came down and the Soviet Union broke up
6. Persian Gulf War

Page 120 Answers will vary.

Page 121
1. a.   5. Office of Homeland Security
2. governor   6. true
3. Answers will vary. 7. c.
4. false

Page 122
1. He was the first African American to become president of Harvard Law School's journal and the United States.
2. mandatory healthcare for children
3. to remove them over a 16-month period

Pages 123–124
1. d.   5. c.   9. d.   13. c.   17. b.
2. a.   6. a.   10. b.   14. d.   18. d.
3. b.   7. c.   11. a.   15. a.   19. a.
4. a.   8. c.   12. b.   16. c.   20. c.